Fibro and Fabulous

Written By

Author Kimberley LB (Kimberley Linstruth-Beckom)

Fibro and Fabulous

ISBN: 978-0-578-04579-5

First edition, December 2009

Introduction

The layout of this book will be set up much like it is on the blog *Fibro and Fabulous*. You will not see a contents page to this book because the entries are as random as the blog. Most subjects will not be grouped together because of this randomness. I wanted to have this book as close to the original form as much as possible.

Blogs are like journals in that you write what comes to mind at the time. This book is set up a lot like that. Each entry will have the trademark *Stay fabulous!* ending and will have a date that signifies when it first appeared on the blog. Some of the entries have been updated for the sole purpose of giving the most current information available on the disease. Not all blog entries will appear in this book. I have only added the ones that were the most popular to readers.

There is also a lot of new stuff, and these entries do not have a date on the top of the page. These never made it to the blog. Some of the new topics that appear in this book are ones that I shy away from in normal conversations. These topics are controversial in nature and can cause a nostril or two to flare. The subject of politics is one, and you will see a little of that here.

Other entries never made it because I didn't have enough research on the topic. I will only discuss a topic that I've researched thoroughly for all of you. I feel that it is unfair, otherwise, to talk about a subject that I know little about.

There are other subjects in this book that offer a fresh look to matters that I've already discussed in prior books and blogs. I feel that if you look at something from different perspectives long enough, you will find what works best for you. This is why I've added a little more on certain subjects for all of you.

There are also entries that contain new ideas all together. These entries are from new information, clinical trials, and also from recent news articles. They will have a bit of my signature commentary.

After long and careful consideration, I decided to put the blog in book form. I wanted to make sure it is readily available in all formats so people can have some daily inspiration at their fingertips when their computer is not handy.

I hope you enjoy how the book has been put together, as well as, enjoy reading it! I know I've had a lot of fun putting it together for you.

Kimberley

Fibro and Fabulous

Wednesday, August 27, 2008

What is Fibro and Fabulous?

It never really dawned on me to do an actual blog about having Fibromyalgia. I've written two books on the subject since my diagnoses, but I never really thought about taking the subject further than the form of a book. Looking back at the whole thing, I realized that it was just silly not to. And now, the blog *Fibro and Fabulous* is born. Funny thing about this whole situation is that that's kind of how my books got published in the first place, I wasn't really thinking about it lol!

Having said that, I also got the idea from looking at what is ahead for the month of September. The week of September 8-14, is Invisible Illness Awareness Week. Frankly, I can't think of a better illness than Fibromyalgia to talk about since it has been an invisible illness for a little over two centuries.

Researchers have found information on the syndrome in books dating back to the 18th century and some have even found references in the Bible at or around 4 BC. Most doctors of today didn't (and some still don't) recognize Fibromyalgia as an actual illness until the FDA approved the medicine Lyrica. That's pretty sad, but true. I remember getting misdiagnosed for years because my doctors simply didn't want to admit to the fact that they had no idea what I had, nor did they want to label it Fibromyalgia.

There is a wonderful site out there that is making the month of September a month to remember all of your friends and loved ones that suffer from an invisible illness. A huge number of illnesses today are invisible. Unfortunately, that makes the person suffering from it *not* look sick. I'm glad this gal, Lisa Copen, founder of *Rest Ministries*, is doing this.

I will be doing as much blogging as I can on *Fibro and Fabulous* about the chronic condition Fibromyalgia, as well as, Chronic Fatigue. Some of the topics I will cover are advice for sufferers, how your family can cope when you become diagnosed, my thoughts on what caregivers may go through with a tough bird like me, and finally, how to live with the illness and still feel fabulous. For any of you who have read my books, you know that part of being fabulous will also deal with your relationships with others, like your children and your mate...especially your mate! We'll get into the territory of my book about intimacy here folks, and I promise it will be clean conversation, but this kind of topic is definitely not for kids. So I'll make sure that a warning of some kind is either in my title or in the first paragraph of the particular blog.

I hope you will enjoy reading Fibro and Fabulous.

For now, take good care of yourselves and I will chat with you soon!

Stay Fabulous!
Love and friendship,

Kimberley

One of the things I'm often asked is, "Kim, how do you find the energy to have kids with your condition?" For me, having a second wasn't a problem, I already had one before diagnoses, so I tried to deal with all of the stuff that goes with them as best as I could.

Yes, sometimes it's not a picnic. Sometimes it can be downright frustrating to find the energy and time to get every task done during the day. You can go crazy running all around your house with winter coats and boots because your kids think you are just playing with them, when in fact, all you want to do is throw out the garbage.

But having children is fun too. There has been many times where my daughters have reminded me that there is more to life than cleaning a toilet bowl. The best times I've had are when I'm playing with them, giving them a bath, and rocking them to sleep. It's at those times where I can let my hair down and just relax right along with them.

I truly feel blessed to have them in my life because they help me deal with my fibromyalgia sometimes better than I do myself. Children are very sensitive by nature, and at times, they know something is wrong with you before you do. My oldest, Brittanny is very good at knowing when I need to take a break because she will ask me if I'd like to play cards with her. I tend to stop what I'm doing at that point so I can make a mental note as to how my body really feels. If I notice a little more fatigue than normal, I will stop and play *Go Fish* with her.

Olivia, my youngest, is a bit different. She is just a toddler and can't put her feeling into words yet, but she can still find a way to stop Mommy dead in her tracks. All she has to do is let me know that she is tired and it's off to the rocker we go. The rocking chair is where she and I can spend a little down time while getting in a little rest too.

It pains me to see so many people with fibromyalgia deciding not to have children based on what they have been told. Some feel that their medication will render them too sick to take care of children, while others feel their physical pain may hamper them from being able to pick their child up. I've read just about as many reasons from people *not* to have children with their illness, as I've personally found reasons *to* have children in your life.

Make no mistake, if you personally feel that you cannot handle a child due to illness, then by all means, you should not have one. For those of you that are out there still wondering whether or not it is possible, it is-- I'm living proof.

It is best to seek the advice of your medical provider first before you consider having a child, but once he/she gives you the go ahead, there are many things you can do to help yourself along the way.

Vitamins are a great way to help you with energy and nutrients that you and baby to be need. A diet rich in complex carbohydrates, fruits, vegetables, diary, and meats will help to keep you and baby active. Rest when you need it-- even if it's in the middle of the day because you may need a little stamina for the evening hours. Finally, any feeding, bathing, or carrying aides you need to help you care for your little one are worth the investment-- don't let anyone tell you otherwise.

Life with a baby can be rewarding, but at times, Mommy needs to think of herself just so she can keep caring for baby. It's okay to take naps when you need to and it's okay to purchase things that will help you care for your baby. I remember a few times when people would look at me funny and say, "Do you really need that?" My answer was, "Yes." because I knew that I'd be taking care of the children 90% of the time by myself. If I'm going to be doing that, I will need help where I can get it and for me, feeding aides, like pillows, sleeping aides, like a portable bassinet, and a small bathing tub that could fit in the kitchen sink, helped me.

I've talked about the feeding pillow I used in a latter entry, so I'll just discuss the bassinet and tub here. The portable bassinet was great because I could easily move it from room to room when Olivia was sleeping. I also liked it because she could sleep right next to me at night for feeding time. Having her in the bassinet helped me with my sleep because I tend to be a very light sleeper when my children are sleeping next to me. I'm a fan of co-sleeping because of my illness, but it can be a double-edged sword when you are a light sleeper. Every whimper, cry, kick, or elbow will wake me up and that's not always so good.

Bath time with Brittanny was not always fun while she was growing up. Keeping my knees on a hard surface for any period of time was becoming increasingly difficult with my fibromyalgia. My knees would ache, sometimes I would get sharp pains, and other times, my feet would fall asleep all together. When she was very young, they did not have the best tools around for bath time like they do now. I used to have to get help from others when I gave her a bath. One of us, be it my mother or husband, would hold her while the other bathed her.

There were times when I would have to ask my husband to bath her all by himself because I didn't have the strength in my knees or my hands. He always was happy to oblige because it gave him the time he needed to bond with Brittanny. Olivia is a bit different. I'm the one who is mostly home, so I am the main caregiver. I still have help because my oldest is good with fetching the towels and also entertaining her sister when it comes time to rinse out her hair.

Sometimes, however, I need a little extra help. Right now I use the sink to bath Olivia because she still fits, but soon, there will come a time when I can't do that anymore and I will have to rely on aides like little tubs and seats specifically designed for the bath tub. There are many different kinds out on the market today and most are available in your local baby store or department store. I like the seats because it gives a toddler support to sit upright.

My bathroom is situated where my toilet seat is right next to the tub and this works out well for me when I need to sit so I can rest my legs. If this is not the case for you, you can remedy the problem with a rubber bath mat and several bath towels. This gives you quite a bit of support so your knees won't be so painful from kneeling on a hard surface. The bath mat is also another great safety feature in aiding against slips and falls.

Having children in your life can be loads of fun, regardless of whether they are yours or not. If you do decide to take the baby plunge and you have a chronic illness, know that there are many resources to help you out. These are just a few suggestions and I'll discuss more as my blog and book develops.

Stay Fabulous!

Love and friendship,

Kimberley

Fibro and Fabulous

An article posted in the Huffington Post for September 21, 2009, has got me thinking about politics. http://www.huffingtonpost.com/tamar-abrams/national-health-care-maki_b_292237.html I'm not one to really talk about politics. It was beat into me as a little kid that politics was a dirty word and *no one* should ever knowingly engage in a conversation about it. I was never sure why, when young, I just knew never to do it.

Government run health care has gotten me to think, though, and when I start to think, I just can't help but share it. With that, I'd like to share my views about the health care business, yes, that's right, I said business.

In my opinion, anything that advertises, receives money from individuals, and is on the stock market, is a business. Let's call a spade, a spade. Generally, a business has one major goal in mind, making money for shareholders. Health care is no different. Yes, there are some people out there who started their business with the full intent of helping people, but those people are few and far between the bunch that want to lace their pockets.

Is this harsh? Perhaps, but I've become desensitized to the money grabbers. You see, I don't think someone should have to decide between putting food on the table or going to the doctor. I also believe that one should not have to go bankrupt because they are sick. Over priced bills can make a healthy person depressed, imagine what it does to the ill. I know I may be preaching to the choir, here, but you can see that this topic is very near and dear to me.

What I'm not desensitized about, is the fact that these companies need to be overseen by someone who does not have a vested interest in whether or not they succeed. Should that mean the government? You bet! Am I an American who believes in freedom all the way down to what I pay for? You bet! But, I also believe that a cap should be put on things that everyone in the United States deserves.

You see, when a company starts to charge a ridiculous amount for health care that I can't afford, I have to go without. Is that American? I say no. That's capitalism, and all capitalism does is allow the richer people more freedoms and perks than the not so rich. Sorry, if there is a price attacked, that's not freedom in my book.

For over 40 years we have heard people on the hill tell us that health care needs to be reformed, but they have not offered to start changing it. I truly hope that President Obama gets to pass health care reform because this country needs it. If nothing gets passed now-- that's okay because sooner or later, something will have to get passed. Big businesses need money to stay afloat and if more and more people can not afford health care, there may not be anyone left to charge their taxes and bills to. Everyone will either be too sick, or worse, dead, to pay up.

Stay Fabulous!

Love and friendship,

Kimberley

Sunday, August 31, 2008

Being Intimate On Relationships

Okay, hopefully most of you reading this have read my prior blog and know that some of my posts, though clean in wording, won't be a good read for kids. This will be one of those kinds of posts. Now, having said that, I feel better that you are forewarned and we can get to the subject at hand.

Relationships are hard enough without adding the extra burden of Fibro, but what can one do when *Fibromyalgia and Sex Can Be A Pain In The Neck?* Well, the first thing to do is to talk about it. I know that sounds too simple and you all may think I'm just plain off my rocker, but think about it for a second. How many of you out there sweep your pain under the rug, shrug it off, and then proceed to go about your day like nothing is wrong? How many people do you "do" that too? Do you do it with your co-workers? How about your friends? Do you do it to your partner?

I know I've done it with all of the above because I felt that my pain wasn't important at the time. But really, how silly is that? If I'm *important* in my co-workers, friends, and partner's lives, then my feelings of being in pain are important. So shrugging it off as if it were nothing is well, like saying *I'm nothing and not important.*

Frankly, I know that that statement couldn't possibly be true. And it's simply because I know I matter to people-- just as you matter to the people in your life.

Talking about your everyday pain really is important because it will give you and your partner a barometer of your *good* and *bad* days. You then both will be able to tell when a flare is coming, why it might have happened, and what it may have been caused by.

Not all flares can be determined, though, and this depends on your actual Fibro condition, however. Some *CAN* be prevented, and using this simple method works well. If you and your partner can get a general idea of why you may hurt, intimacy may not be so foreign in your lives as a couple. It can become fun instead of just being another thing that causes you *a pain in the neck.*

I discuss this topic in my book called *Fibromyalgia and Sex Can Be A Pain In The Neck...and back and shoulders.* It is available at many sites online, including Amazon, Barnes and Noble, and Borders, but I've always suggested to purchase it at Lulu.com because that site is a wonderful one for finding new voices.

The book covers the topic of intimacy thoroughly and goes into greater detail as to what has worked for my husband and me. For now, however, I must bid you goodbye and I will leave you by saying, take care of yourselves!

Stay Fabulous!

Love and friendship,

Kimberley

Some of you may wonder what my thoughts on medication are in relation to sexual health. Personally, I have not taken a medication that affects my sexuality and my views are rather simple when it comes to this subject...

Start a log for yourself that contains how you feel and what type of side effects you may be able to attribute to the medication you are on. Once you have sufficient information, about a month's worth of logs, take it to your doctor so the both of you can discuss what is going on.

If you feel that your medications for sleep and depression are robbing you of your most intimate moments, tell your doctor. Most people, I know, do not like to discuss this subject with their doctors. Some feel that they should just be thankful that some of their symptoms are being alleviated. Others are embarrassed.

No matter what you are feeling at the time, try and talk with him/her. Chances are good that they will understand what you are going through and suggest another alternative. I was lucky in the sense that I did not take any medication that affected my sexual drive, but I did take some medication that had some undesirable side effects.

One medication left me very dizzy after taking it. I made sure to keep a log just to be certain that the medicine was the culprit, and then voiced my concerns with my doctor at the next visit. He in turn prescribed an alternative and this medicine worked much better.

Stay Fabulous!

Love and friendship,

Kimberley

Monday, September 8, 2008

Getting to Fabulous

Getting to *Fabulous* can seem like a daunting and difficult task for anyone who suffers from Fibromyalgia. The fatigue alone can make everything seem hard. But somehow, everyone of us with this debilitating syndrome manage lives with a job, kids, a partner, hobbies, pets, and anything else you might think of that would be included in a life. We do it simply because we were people before we got diagnosed and we are most certainly people after that. It's finding that happy medium between illness and life that can really make a person wrestle with priorities.

I discuss in great detail a lot of that turmoil that I went through when first diagnosed in my book **The Fibro Hand**, and I'll share a bit of it here, as well as, some of my other thoughts.

I was always hard-working by nature. And anyone looking at me probably would probably say I was a kid that felt I had something to prove. I was constantly over doing it and pushing the envelope. I was that kid with a constant sling for my sprained and strained joints. My classmates in middle school used to take bets as to whether a school mate, Matt, or I would show up with crutches on a given week. So, it's with that, that I can definitely say I started to *work* through pain at quite an early age.

My danger-prone pre-teens years made it very hard for me to distinguish *aches and pains* from actual Fibro flares. They seemed pretty similar to me. It really wasn't until after giving birth to my first child that I experienced some really crappy days where I just plain couldn't move my fingers in the morning. Even then, at age 28, I just tossed it off as nothing more than being tired from sleepless nights and long work days.

When I turned 30, and got promoted to a *real* management job at a retail department store, things started to change. Middle management was a position I held since the age of 16, so I knew what to expect. The uppers wanted a lot of long hours from you that entailed a lot of stocking of merchandise. This new position was a bit different. I was doing a major amount of walking in the store because the upper management felt that a presence was needed to boost sales and morale.

The particular store I was in, was a mall store and it had two floors. Now, to make a long story, short, I was walking anywhere from 5-15 miles a day during my shifts at work. My knees were literally killing me. I went to the doctor to find out what was wrong, and so began the process of figuring out what I had, and what to do about it.

After the diagnoses of Fibromyalgia, I started to read

everything I could on the subject and I tried to meet as many people as I could that had it. I wanted to beat this thing that was robbing me of the life and job I had.

One particular book took my be surprise. It dealt with Fibromyalgia in a whole new way. The author explained that food and other natural approaches would help manage the pain. This book called **Fibromyalgia, A Natural Approach,** talked about a "detox" program where you eliminate food that cause problems in your diet. I was ecstatic and felt in control again of my life because I now had an idea and a plan to help me to feel better.

After reading this book, I started to keep a journal of what I ate and how I felt afterwards. I tracked whether my ankles swelled, if I was tired, or if I had a burst of energy. It worked so well, I also did this for my activities so I keep track of those too.

I wrote in this journal faithfully for one week, at first, and then I started tracking it off and on for a couple of months. Once my regular foods and routines were tracked, I continued the journal for any new activities and foods. This gave me a great record of what worked well for my body and what caused flares.

Now, I'm not a doctor, so I must stress that getting yourself checked out by one before you start any regimen. This journal, however, helped my doctor and I to communicate better. I was able to use the journal as a tool to let him know what helped and what didn't.

Fibromyalgia is a tricky syndrome to diagnose because its symptoms can look like Lyme disease, MS, or even RA, to name a few. It is best to get tested so your doctor can rule out other disease. Self medicating can be self defeating if you don't know what you are up against.

I hope these tips will help you get closer to fabulous. A journal may seem like a daunting task, especially to some who don't like to write, but it can truly aid you in feeling better. The journal does not have to be long or even formatted for anyone to read. As long as you can read what you have written, it will serve its purpose. Feeling fabulous despite your condition is essential to making you feel better-- at least in my opinion. It is with that, I say, take care of yourselves until next time...

Stay Fabulous!

Love and friendship,

Kimberley

Tuesday, September 9, 2008

The Guilt Factor

Warning: This blog entry is not a suitable read for children. It contains a mature topic.

Okay, now that the warning is out of the way, I'd like to discuss in today's blog, *The Guilt Factor* which is a topic I go into great detail about in my book, *Fibromyalgia and Sex Can Be a Pain In The Neck... and back and shoulders.* I also have an announcement about a special contest that I'm running in honor of National Invisible Illness Awareness Week. I'll discuss that contest in better detail at the end of this blog, but for now, let's talk about our *pleasure to please people.*

I've always thought that my *pleasure to please* can get the best of me at times. I'm a Mom, so I go out of my way to please, and I'm sure all you Moms out there know what I mean by that, but we all-- whether we are Moms or not-- try to please the people we love by doing things for them.

I'm sure that every one of you will agree (unless you really, really enjoy housework) that cleaning out the cat box, taking out the trash, or cleaning the toilet, are not things we enjoy doing. But we do these things because we love the people and pets we have in our lives. These things, of course, don't always have to be done by you, the sufferer, because, well let's face it-- there are days when even opening up a jar just seems impossible. It's at those times that you delegate tasks out.

But what happens with your *pleasure to please* when it comes to you and your partner's intimacy? I'm sure you've felt like me and you've had it on your brain some nights. However, intimacy can wind up sounding too much like an everyday task when you hurt. Then, in comes *The Guilt Factor* when this happens. Let's get even more frank, here, by saying how can one please their partner and themselves with a little intimacy, and still be able to walk in morning? You can do this by getting a little selfish. The use of the mantra, *It's all about me* is all you need.

Now, before any of you think that I'm totally crazy-- let me explain what I mean. My husband and I got a little creative with my daily fibro journal and decided to expand my list to include what works for my body even when it comes to intimacy.

When you start a list for intimacy, you'll become even more aware of your body and how it works for you. The more aware you are, the more *about me* you become.

Once you have figured out what works, *The Guilt Factor* can then go where it belongs-- right out of your life. You'll finally be able to do what you wanted to in the first place-- please your partner. The only difference now is that you will be trying new things. Incorporating more massage into your intimacy might work for you, for instance, or you might wind up going back to familiar favorites. Either way, your, *it's all about me* mantra will allow you and your partner to have a whole lot of fun.

Stay Fabulous!
Love and friendship,

Kimberley

This article posted for October 2, 2009 goes into great detail as to what medications and conditions cause low or poor libido in woman. It's no surprise that Fibromyalgia makes the list. Medication to treat Fibromyalgia can play a big role in libido for women. The biggest and most common culprit to blame is antidepressant medications. But did you ever think that your allergy, migraine, or birth control pills might be to blame?

http://www.usrecallnews.com/2009/10/decreased-sex-drive-in-women-a-symptom-or-side-effect.html

It's shocking to think that a common over-the-counter medication such as Benadryl could cause low libido, but this article states that the side effects of this common drug can in fact do just that. Worse, it can cause infertility.

I personally avoid Benadryl at all costs. It's not a medication that sets well with me. Call it an allergic reaction, intolerance, or fibro symptoms, my body does not like it. I become very lucid, almost to the point that some would say I'm acting drunk-- not a feeling I care to be in, especially around my children.

If you are concerned about side effects from any of the medications you are taking-- whether they are prescribed or not-- talk to your doctor and even your pharmacist. They often have suggestions and alternatives for unwanted side effects. I would even go so far as to say to stop taking them if you are absolutely sure that the side effects are worse than the condition itself. Just make sure you let your doctor know of your decision so he/she can better assist you.

Medication is tricky for everyone, but especially tricky for Fibromyalgia sufferers due to heightened reactions. Some patients, like me, find it extremely hard to take anything, even a common over-the-counter remedy. Just remember, you know your body better than anyone else, so if you notice something wrong, there probably is.

Stay Fabulous!

Love and friendship,

Kimberley

Fibro and Fabulous

Thursday, September 11, 2008

<u>Stress Busters</u>

Hey everyone! Sorry I didn't have a chance to post yesterday. I was "busy" tending to my 8 month old who was very clingy yesterday. She's most definitely a Mama's girl and has a very hard time separating from me. It's kind of funny because, in a sense, she seems to know when I'm about to have a flare since she cries for me to pick her up. Now, some of you are probably thinking I'm nuts by saying that because she's just a little baby and how "sensitive" can a baby be-- right? Well the answer to that is simple, babies are pretty sensitive. They can be just as sensitive to their caregivers as a pet would be and when they "react" to you like that, it can actually be beneficial. Sometimes just holding a child or a pet or even tending a to a garden or aquarium can relieve stress. It's a pretty old and known fact and that's going to be the topic of discussion for today.

I've had pets in my home all of my life. Both sets of grandparents had dogs and my parents had cats. I remember having a bit of trouble when I was little with the pet hair because I was allergic, but it never stopped me from loving animals of all kinds.

As an adult, I now have 13 pets that are the topic of conversation in my blogs every now and then. My two cats were in the literal sense of being stray.

Diamond was an unwanted and abused kitten before I had him. When I first got him, he hated men. At the time, that was fine with me, of course, because I was getting over a bad relationship and I hated them too lol! But, after a while, he grew to tolerate men once my husband started feeding him.

Diamond did a few other special things once he started to see that I was getting ill. He started to follow me around the house during my really bad days and would even move my daughter's toys away from my walking path so I would not have to bend. Diamond also learned how to open cabinets to get out his canned food and hair brush. He is very sensitive to my illness, a love to have in my life, and a great stress reliever because when I take the time to be with him, I'm forgetting my own troubles for a bit.

Topaz showed up on my doorstep about two years ago and is my other great love. She is my lap cat who doesn't mind being brushed (unlike Diamond) and just wants as much attention and love she can get from you. She is the cat that will fight Diamond to get a better seat by my bedside just so she can be there until I'm well enough to get up. She is another wonderfully sensitive cat and is yet another love in my life.

My other pets are two African- clawed frogs and several tropical fish. Fish are another wonderful way to relieve stress-- believe it or not. Some of them that

I've had over the years can get excited to see you, just like any dog or cat would when they see their caregivers come home, and some will even eat out of your hand. But the best thing about fish is that you can have calmness in your life by just watching them swim. In other words, they could act as a meditative tool for you to help you relax your sometimes clouded, busy mind.

I have a tank in both of my daughters' rooms and a tank in the family room that I love to look at when I'm tending to the children, or when I'm by myself. It's a great way to relax and the fish won't mind because they are like all pets-- they are there to be loved.

Children are another great love of mine and they can also be great stress busters. A child can say some of the most profound things if you are lucky enough to listen. They also don't seem to care as to whether you can walk or not either. My 7 year old daughter will look at me after I've told her I can't play ball with her and say, "Okay Mommy, then let's play cards instead."

Life is pretty simple for them and we as adults could learn a very valuable lesson from them by finding what relieves our stress and just taking some time to relieve it. I'm glad that I have so many animals, children, and even a husband in my life to help me remember how to relieve mine. Here's to finding yours!

Stay Fabulous!

Love and friendship,

Kimberley

Fibro and Fabulous

Monday, September 29, 2008

Fibromyalgia and Pregnancy

I touched on the subject of kids in the previous blog as being a great source of stress relief. They are innocent and give unconditional love. And children are wonderful to have in your life regardless of whether you have a chronic condition or not. I can't tell you how many forum and chat rooms I've been in that cater to people suffering from Fibromyalgia where the subject of children comes up, but there are a lot, and the topic that seems the most interesting to many is pregnancy.

Some of you who have recently had a baby know that there was a baby boom in 2007. I missed that boom by one month and had my littlest one this past January, but I, like all the other mothers to be, was very eager to find out as much information as I possibly could on pregnancy and Fibromyalgia.

I was diagnosed in late 2005, which was well after my first pregnancy, and I must admit that I was a bit leery of what might happen to me and a new baby due to my chronic illness, so any information would have been a welcoming comfort to me.

Fibromyalgia is still considered a relatively new syndrome and only recently has an FDA approved medicine, so information and studies can be hard to come by in research, however, I have found some studies relating to Fibromyalgia and pregnancy, and the facts that I have found are pretty positive.

First, I must stress that I am not a doctor and I cannot diagnose or treat anyone's medical condition. You must see your own doctor and discuss pregnancy with them. But if you are afraid of trying to have children because of Fibromyalgia, please feel rest assured that studies show that this debilitating condition might not be passed on to your children.

Dr. Mark Pellegrino stated in an article taken from the *National Fibromyalgia Association* in August of 2005 that the baby has a greater vulnerability of getting it because of the genetic component, but that is the only risk to the fetus.

It is true that some doctors have stated that babies can be affected by the prescribed drugs and herbal supplements of some patients suffering from Fibromyalgia. And most will caution women to go drug free before, during, and for breast feeding mothers, after pregnancy, but these side effects are shown to be from the prescribed drugs and those effects usually happen during the first four to six weeks of pregnancy when a baby is most vulnerable.

Some of the research I've read about supplements can vary greatly from doctor to doctor and this is where your own GP, OBGYN, and Fibromyalgia specialist (usually a rheumatologist) should be involved to help you sort out what is best for you yourself.

I had decided to go drug free myself a few months before trying to get pregnant with the help and guidance of my doctors. By drug free, I mean getting off of all supplements except a prenatal, and stopping my use of Advil and Tylenol.

It was hard in the beginning, but once I became pregnant, my Fibro symptoms were not that bad. Some even became non-existent. One study has shown this to be true for pregnant Fibromyalgia sufferers. They seemed to be symptom free for about the first six to seven months of pregnancy.

I will stress that there is a very recent study done by Dr. Karen M. Schafer that contradicts this finding. Her study findings are similar to a study done in Norway in the 1970's. This study was done with only nine mothers that ranged in age of 26-36 and these mothers already had a previous pregnancy before diagnoses.

She states that mothers had more fatigue and pain in the last trimester and they also found it very difficult to breastfeed due to soreness and stiffness of their joints. Some also had a problem with sore nipples. This may be common with all mothers, but for Fibromyalgia sufferers and mothers with arthritis, it may be more common, according to the La Leche League.

La Leche League's article states that some medications and steroids can cause the mother to have a problem with yeast infections, and if you are suffering from cracked or bleeding nipples, you should consider it to be thrush and get medical advice to treat it.

Now, studies are just that-- studies. Believe me when I tell you that some of the information out there can make your head spin. Mine went into overdrive when I read all the controversy, but remember, FM is still a new disease. The best thing you can do for yourself is to get a support system going because you are going to need it. The old saying, *It takes a village to raise a child,* is so true, and a lot of people, I'm sure, will be willing to help you.

I remember wanting to do it all and being just way too tired to do anything. I allowed myself a lot of time to rest and asked for a lot of people to help me clean my house and do laundry.

I also looked for support with mothers who breastfed their babies and suffered from FM. There are many forums out there that have a dedicated page for this, but the La Leche League gals were one of my favorite groups.

I must stress that making the decision to breast or bottle feed is a very personal matter and some people may make you feel bad if you can't breastfeed your baby. That is just sad. There are a lot of selfish and cruel people in the world who do things to make themselves feel better. Don't let them fool you.

Always remember that you are the mother and you love your child. If you are making the best decision you can possibly make for the *both* of you, then it's a good decision that was made out of love. I bottle fed my first and breast fed my second and there are wonderful perks with both, so don't let someone else make your decision for you, and don't feel guilty about it either.

There are so many other tips that I have found that work well when it comes to holding and feeding your baby that I'll be discussing in further blogs. The information I have is just too much to condense into one blog. Most of what I have collected will be going into my new book which I'll announce to all of my readers here...

I am going to write another book on Fibromyalgia and this one will be on my pregnancy. I will talk about tips and tricks, and of course, my trials with Fibro. I will also discuss how to talk to your children about your chronic condition.

Children are truly wonderful and will give you great blessings of joy in your life. They can help you stay young and also remind you how to be *fabulous*. Take care of yourselves, until next time.

Stay Fabulous!
Love and friendship,

Kimberley

This story just made the news yesterday, September 18, 2009. It is a story that has me wondering why the pharmaceutical companies are not being looked at as part of the problem for drug misuse in this country.

Every time you turn on the TV, open up your email, or drive by a billboard on the highway, there's at least one ad for a drug. Why do these companies even have to advertise to us, the consumer, when your doctor needs to make the final decision as to what medication is best for you? The doctor writes the scripts-- not the patient!

Make no mistake, I am not condoning or dismissing what this girl has done. In fact, the way this report is reading, the girl did not publicly give her side of the story.

http://www.jsonline.com/news/crime/59752542.html

We may never know what truly happened in the death of her child, but we do know that she suffered from Fibromyalgia. She also had many problems with prescription drugs due to her health conditions.

This does not paint a pretty picture for Fibro sufferers any way you slice it because we are not drug addicts. Most of us hate doctors and I know that I can comfortably say that we don't like taking medication of any kind. I've had many of my readers tell me this.

Fibro sufferers are faced with a lot. We have doctors that think we are crazy and will push any kind of pill on us just to get us out of their office. We have people in our lives who think we are not sick. They think we are making up excuses not to work, or play, or whatever.

All of these things are misunderstandings that can turn into out and out lies if the medical community continues to deal with people by just giving them a pill. It's not right to treat people this way. Most of us are genuine with genuine problems. We go to a doctor for answers to our symptoms.

Yes, doctors don't know everything about us and our bodies, that's why they run tests. Most people still feel that a doctor knows more than they do about health. They trust in what the doctor has to say. However, when a doctor would rather delve out medication like its Halloween, rather than get to the root of the problem, a patient really should take notice. We are not kids, we don't need a lollipop. We need understanding as Fibromyalgia sufferers.

Stay Fabulous!

Love and friendship,

Kimberley

Thursday, October 9, 2008

The Diet Debate

There are two studies out there stating that Fibro sufferers could gain relief from their symptoms by changing their diet to mostly raw vegetables, or in other words, going vegan. One study is from Finland and the other is from North Carolina and both had their subjects eat a diet rich in raw vegetables and low on salt for about three months.

These two studies are wonderful news because it shows that Fibromyalgia can be relieved naturally. I've always believed this, but I'm not a vegan. Don't get me wrong-- fruits and veggies are very important in the diet, but I also believe that the other food groups are just as important for optimal health. I try to incorporate a balance of every food group in all of my meals while eating healthy snacks in between.

Even though I eat meat, you may wonder if I've added or cut anything out of my diet to help to ease the pain. I have, I've cut out what my oldest daughter and I call *fake food*. *Fake food* is food that has been altered by chemicals and/or refining. About 80 percent of the foods you find in the supermarket today have been altered in some way according to Christine Craggs-Hinton, author of ***Fibromyalgia, A Natural Approach***.

I truly believe she's right because I've read the labels of most of the boxed and canned foods out there in the isles and a good majority are filled with chemical ingredients that I can't pronounce. That's pretty sad considering I was an English Major in college. Not all of the labels contain bad things and some of that boxed and canned stuff is actually real food. So how does this sufferer tell the difference without having to read *War and Peace*? I went *organic*.

The word *organic* today is just another term for *real food*, as my oldest daughter and I put it. A lot of organic food isn't as expensive as one might think. I have found many products that are at a reasonable price at some regular supermarkets and some at organic food stores like **Trader Joe's** and **Whole Foods**.

Consumers are demanding better quality products and that's driving down some of the costs. Another thing that markets are doing to lower cost is to buy from local farms. Lower transportation costs, lowers the cost of the food.

I go into great detail about good organic products to buy in my book **The Fibro Hand**, but a basic rule of thumb is to just read the labels. If the list of ingredients is long, chances are pretty good that it's not organic.

Good meats are easily found by buying ones that contain no hormones. If it is chicken products like eggs or stock, the best kind to get are free-range. Free- range means that the animal was not locked up in a cage when it was laying eggs or when it was feeding itself-- in other words-- its life was good.

There is quite a bit of controversy surrounding free-range chickens, as well as, hormone-free dairy products. Some people believe that this is just a ploy that farmers use to raise prices. There may be a lot of controversy, but this fibromite will continue to buy better quality products until I'm thoroughly convinced otherwise. I have seen, first hand, how different my oldest daughter reacts emotionally to lower grade meat and dairy products-- it's not pretty.

Fish also is healthier for you if you buy wild caught instead of farm raised. Farm raised fish live in crowded quarters which can make them unhealthy for many reasons. One in particular, is mercury levels. According to an NPR radio news report, some scientists fear that fish living in such close quarters may make mercury levels rise in certain fish. I have not seen any more research or reports that confirm or deny these findings. If I do, you, my dear readers, will be the first to know.

Fruits and vegetables that are safe to eat can be purchased inexpensively too. You do not need to go all organic. For instance, some fruits, like bananas, have a thick casing that covers the fruit. Pesticides won't be able to penetrate this casing, so it is okay to go for the non-organic variety in this case. The list of must haves for organic is quite small. Oranges, grapefruits, green beans (fresh and frozen), grapes, plums, apples, lettuce, strawberries, wheat, cauliflower, and pears absorb more pesticides than most other fruits, vegetables, and grain, according to the USDA.

Eating well is a lifestyle choice and it can help with your Fibro pain if you try to eliminate chemicals and preservatives that do not react well with your body. Each person with Fibromyalgia is different, so getting a journal together to record your reactions is important.

There is still very little research being done in the field of diet. The research is still not definitive and tends to run one-sided. In some cases, the studies seem bias and contradicting. For instance, one study said a glass of wine a day is healthy, while another said it is not. Both studies were done to determine if cancer risk could be lowered, with or without, wine intake. One can only hope that there will be further studies on the diet so we sufferers have more information to help us in managing our pain.

Stay Fabulous!
Love and friendship,

Kimberley

The birthing experience can be fun and exciting. As a first-time mom you have no idea what to expect. If you've already had one pregnancy under your belt, you feel a little less nervous, but each pregnancy and labor is different.

Pregnancy cravings, body changes, mood swings, and bloating are all part of the package of having a baby. If you suffer from Fibromyalgia, you may have a few more symptoms than these common ones. Your doctor may or may not keep you on your medication regimen. That, of course, is up to your doctor and it should be documented when you get to the hospital for delivery, but did you ever think that your hospital might call Child Protective Services on you if you have been taking prescribed medication?

A forum geared towards Fibro sufferers has a section dedicated to Fibromyalgia and pregnancy. http://www.mdjunction.com/forums/fibromyalgia-discussions/general-support/844514-fibromyalgia-and-pregnancy

In the forum, it states that a mom had to go through a very difficult experience because her doctor was not present in the beginning to aide in the birth of her child. She also states that the hospital called in Child Protective Services on her because they believed that the baby was a drug abused baby. She, of course, was not abusing her doctor prescribed medication.

The doctor had a watchful eye on her and the baby at each prenatal visit.

Unfortunately for her, the medications she was taking were not on her chart, an error was made. When she questioned the hospital, she was then told that she "was not the norm". Apparently at that hospital, most of the babies born with drugs in their system came from a drug addicted mother.

This information is shocking, and I know it cannot truly be confirmed, but regardless of whether or not the actual incident is valid, something like this can and probably does happen. It is possible due to human error, that certain things might not make it onto your chart.

When I gave birth to my first daughter, I explained to the nurse that I was deathly allergic to penicillin. The nurse looked at my chart and then nervously said to me, "Well that is good to know because we were about to give you a derivative of it." That was a scary thought and it could have been a fatal one if I chose to stay silent.

What I learned from that whole experience was that you can never say something enough times. It's important to make sure everyone has the information they need to care for you properly. Repeating yourself is a good thing-- even if it's annoying to do so.

I wore a bracelet that stated I was allergic to penicillin with my second and made sure that my allergies made it to my chart. If I were in this mother's case, I probably would have told everyone, including the janitor, what prescribed medicines I was on and I would be crossing my legs till the doctor got there.

Perhaps that humor may sound a bit harsh, but when it comes to having someone present that knows what is going on, verses someone who doesn't, and lives depend on that knowledge, I will wait for as long as it takes.

Stay Fabulous

Love and friendship,

Kimberley

The Internet is a great wealth of information for anyone who wants to research a disease. Many of my friends have done this (including me) countless numbers of times. We all do it for comfort-- whether it's to pass the time between doctor's visits by dismissing a terrible disease we couldn't possibly have, or we want to find out how bad our disease is once we are diagnosed.

I remember doing extensive research before and after my diagnoses of Fibromyalgia. I scared myself silly because I would sit for hours in front of the computer going through lists of symptoms for everything from MS to FMS. I wondered if I unknowingly passed anything on to my children too.

Somehow, though, the computer gave me a little comfort. It was like a friend, giving me the truth that I needed to hear. It didn't try and make me feel better by lying to my face with blanket statements. My favorite saying was everything will turn out fine. I didn't need that.

In the same token, though, some sites out there give the good ones a bad name. It is so discouraging to see people write what is supposed to be an informative article on a disease and not follow through with good information. I majored in English at college and was taught that an informative article needs facts to back it up. Those facts need to be researched and cited somewhere in your article too.

This article on Fibromyalgia and pregnancy (http://causesoffibromyalgia.info/pregnant-and-dealing-with-fibromyalgia/) is a classic example of what *not* to do. Sure, it states research in the form of two studies, but it lacks extremely important information. Information like when were the studies done? How many subjects were in these studies? Are there any other studies done that conflict with the findings of these two? The list of questions can go on and on.

A writer has a duty to report *all* the facts, not just the ones that suit opinions or needs. Yes, an article can spark controversy, that's okay, but not when it is at the expense of others. A woman can in fact have less Fibromyalgia symptoms when pregnant and there are certain drugs that a woman can have while pregnant. In fact, there are drugs being tested in clinical trials as we speak for pregnant women who suffer from Fibromyalgia. I've discussed this information in previous blogs and it also appears in this book, so for the sake of not wanting to bore you all to tears, I will not repeat myself.

Articles like these tend to put my blood at a boiling point because I feel no one has a right to an opinion when it comes to writing a factual article. However, I can't stop stupidity. I can only offer some good advice on how to weed through all the garbage out there.

Look for footnotes in the article. If the writer has them, that is a good place to start when looking for the facts of a study. If the writer provided the information on a study, look to see how many people participated. If there were only a few, the study is not all that valid. Did the writer base the entire article on one study? If so, the article is biased to the writer's opinion. Hope this helps.

Stay Fabulous!

Love and friendship,

Kimberley

I don't normally let bad comments get to me. I'm in a business where negative people like to publicly destroy others for their own selfish reasons. Allowing them to see you hurt just adds fuel to their fire, so I don't like to allow them the privilege. The problem with it all, though, is that sometimes your loyal fans will wonder and doubt you if it's not addressed. I can understand this kind of thinking and sympathize with it.

Comments that anyone makes about my writing are always welcome, whether you agree with me or not. But if you disagree with me, please understand that I don't have to cower and crawl underneath a rock somewhere.

I can fully understand that you may not like something that I've said and want everyone to know about it, but in the same token, you also must understand that you are affecting my lively hood for my children when you tell others not to buy my books. I most certainly don't go around telling your boss that you don't perform well, so I honestly expect the same courtesy.

A while back, I had a not so nice comment made about my book, *Fibromyalgia and Sex Can Be a Pain in the Neck....* The gal thought the book did not have enough medical facts in it. She wanted a medical opinion about sex. That is fine. She also thought the book was poorly written. Well, that's fine too. Everyone is entitled to an opinion.

I'd like the gal out there to know that I went to college to learn how to research and write. I have a degree as an English major which allows me to write in any genre-- not just journalism. I'm more than qualified to write a book. I was first published at the age of 9 and that was in 1982, some 27 years ago, another qualification.

My loyal readers know that I am very knowledgeable when it comes to fact finding for Fibromyalgia. I write for them-- not for me. Most of what I do cannot be measured by a dollar amount since I post many, many articles for free for the sufferers out there. When you are putting out more money than you make on your medical bills, spending a few bucks on a book is hard. I get that because I live it.

However, I can understand this gal's side of things. After all, she was able to spring for a book. So, I'd like that gal out to know that I have found an article for her from a doctor that discusses Fibromyalgia and sex if you need a medical doctor to reiterate what I've already discussed in *Fibromyalgia and Sex Can Be a Pain in the Neck...*, you can read it here in today's posting of *Disaboom*.

http://www.disaboom.com/fibromyalgia/fibromyalgia-and-your-sex-life

Now, that that is out of the way, to my dear readers, I hope you can understand my rant and forgive this little burst from me. I know that it is out of character for me, but I want you all to know that I value each and every one of you dearly. I don't want any negativity to come your way. You all have enough negativity to deal with in your lives just by having this beast. It's not fair to have to deal with selfish people too, and this is why I had to address this negative comment.

Stay Fabulous!

Love and friendship,

Kimberley

Tuesday, October 21, 2008

<u>Support System</u>

Today's topic is about having a support system in family, friends, and even co-workers. This subject is very near and dear to me because it was the hardest thing for me to do. I'm very independent to a fault because I was used to being the one to help everyone else out. I was not used to being the one who asked for help.

There were days when I became very discouraged at what I couldn't do anymore. I tried very hard not to express any feelings of discouragement, but at those times, my close friends, co-workers, and family would somehow find a way to pry them out of me. They were all very patient with me, and frankly, I'm not sure I'd be the person I am today if they were not so persistent with me.

See, the hard part for me was asking someone, like my husband for instance, to do something like open up a jar of pickles. I felt that if I was the one who wanted the pickles, I should be the one opening up that jar. Now, I know that using a jar of pickles as an analogy may seem a little weird to people, but it's a good analogy because it seems so trivial. And that's exactly how I felt when I was the one asking for help-- I thought that my asking for help was trivial.

Sometimes help can't wait a day, or two, or twenty, when it comes to things like cooking a meal, or even cleaning a kitchen or bathroom. It was at those times that I had to get past my trivial thinking and actually pursue help from those that cared about me.

What you need from people at any given time can range from moral support to someone making a pot of coffee for you. There are also times that the help won't be exactly what you are looking for. Like say, for instance, someone, who shall remain nameless (he knows who he is) may for some reason decide to dry your delicate lingerie in the dryer so they are ready for you to wear.

It's a nice thought, it really is, but, that may not be the kind of help you are looking for, especially if the dryer has your most prized (and only) Victoria's Secret bra spinning away on the cotton cycle. It is help, though, and that is what you may need on those bad days when you can't walk-- let alone do laundry.

The lesson I've learned the most from all of this, is that communication is key to helping and healing not only yourself, but the person or people who want to help you too. Let them know what you need instead of being tight lipped. After all, they may want to love you back for all the good you've done for them. And that would be just *fabulous*-- wouldn't it?

Stay Fabulous!

Love and friendship,

Kimberley

Friday, October 24, 2008

Plant Some Happiness

When I was young, I remember wanting to have a houseplant in my bedroom. My Mother and Grandmother were happy to oblige my request as long as I was the one watering it. I remember feeling so excited and proud that I was old enough to be able to tend to this little ivy I picked out for my room.

As the weeks went by, I tried to give it everything it needed, but it wasn't fairing very well in my room because of the lack of sun. I had a north facing window and that can be a death sentence to plants that require moderate to full sun. So, my Mother placed the little plant near a better window in the family room and it lasted for a bit of time there until some white flies got a hold of it. I was devastated and swore off gardening for years after that incident.

Many years went by and a friend of mine tried to persuade me into taking up indoor gardening again. I was settled in an apartment with full sun, a perfect environment for houseplants. I told her of my sad ordeal and how I never wanted to go back to gardening again due to my *black* thumb. She decided that she wasn't going to take no for an answer from me and gave me two spider plants as a gift one day.

Well, even though I was hesitant, I graciously took

those plants into my home and gave them a nice comfortable spot near my kitchen window. These plants grew very well, in fact so well, that they are still alive today and have produced many, many offspring that I've proudly raised and given as gifts to other people.

These two plants were the start of a beautiful relationship with anything that grows, and now, my relationship has bloomed into flowering plants, as well as, fruit and vegetable plants. I have so much more confidence in gardening that I experiment with a huge variety of species. In fact, I will try to put anything in a pot to see if it will grow. This is such a fun hobby and I have my friend to thank for this beautiful gift that she has given me.

Now, you are probably wondering what this story, though lovely, has to do with Fibromyalgia. Well, the answer is plenty. Gardening, even if it's only done indoors, is a great stress reliever, and a great source of happiness. There is just something wonderful and humbling about getting your hands dirty. It can put your life into perspective. I feel that putting my hands in soil is like a metaphor in a sense because I'm putting energy and love into something to see if it will grow, just like I put energy and love into trying be fabulous despite my condition.

I touch on houseplants a bit in my book, *The Firbo Hand* where I explain how plants can help you. But my self-discoveries are here in this blog. I hope this encourages some of you to try and plant some happiness for yourselves.

Stay Fabulous!
Love and friendship,

Kimberley

Monday, November 3, 2008

<u>Please Be Kind...Rewind</u>

Something occurred to me the other day about care giving when I was having a discussion with my husband. I call them discussions when something he may be doing is annoying me. And believe me when I tell you, this was a long discussion.

You see, my husband either believes that we have little pixies that clean the bathroom, kitchen, and pick up dirty laundry, or he has a tendency to take me for granted. And since I don't believe that pixies live on Earth, I'm going to go with the later explanation.

Now, don't get me wrong, my husband is a wonderful man, but he's human, and humans tend to forget things. And of course, I can be a pretty good gal and be able to clean house on my good days, but again, I'm only human and my flares prohibit me from doing what I want.

What occurred to me was that he and I have two very different ways of giving help. You see, if someone asks me to do some wash for them, I'll take it upon myself to separate lights, darks, and delicates, check for tough stains, pre-treat, and then proceed to do the wash.

On the other hand, my husband will hear the same task, and put everything together in one load and hit start. Now, both accomplish the same task, in essence, but one may give you pink underwear and baby doll shirts. At least it's done, though, right?

Well, I could say right, but on those days that it happens, I get very frustrated and upset. I feel like it's really my fault that my sweater will better fit my 9 month-old now than me, yet it really wasn't my fault. Then I feel like I just should have done the task myself so I could save all of the aggravation. That really isn't the answer, either.

I like to think of those types of situations as a "Please be kind...Rewind". And what I mean by that is that there are many people out there who love us and try to help us in many ways when they understand what we are going through with the pain of Fibromyalgia.

Sometimes, though, even the ones who seem to understand may slip up and forget how hard life can be for someone who feels like a truck hit them right after they mop a floor.

If this happens, I try and think of a time when that person was understanding and try to calm myself down. In other words-- I rewind. The being kind usually happens later when I'm calm, but you get my point.

So if this ever happens to you, try and think about hitting the rewind button.

Stay Fabulous!
Love and friendship,

Kimberley

Wednesday, November 12, 2008

You Are What You Eat

One of the first things that I did when I got
diagnosed with Fibromyalgia was to go to the local
Borders store and find books on nutrition for Fibro
sufferers. I got home, and then started soaking up the
knowledge.

At first, I couldn't believe what I was reading when I
opened up the food additive section. It was shocking
to see so many things containing things like MSG. I
thought MSG was eliminated from food all together
in the 80's. I remember walking by the Chinese
restaurants when I was young and saw the No MSG
advertising on their store windows. Of course, I
quickly found out how wrong I was when I started to
read food labels.

Food shopping is a whole new adventure for me and
the family because I spend time and label read. We
also tend to go to places like Trader Joe's and Whole
Foods, as opposed to the old stand by food markets,
because I can find much healthier alternatives to the
classic family food additive favorites.

I make a lot of things from scratch now because of
the amount of junk that's in prepared foods. Prep
time for a home cooked meal can sometimes be time
consuming this way. It can also be torture for the

chronically fatigued. So how do you prepare a fabulously healthy meal without zapping your own health in the process? You cheat.

You heard me right, you can cheat. I found through the years that making something quick can be a life saver when it comes to my fibro and fatigue. I've cheated by having already cut up veggies and prepackaged salads in my fridge and freezer along with some canned foods. Now, you might be wondering how I can get away with canned foods when a lot of them out there are filled with too much junk.

In the organic isles of food stores, and in places like Trader Joe's, you can find canned foods that are healthy and contain no preservatives. These canned foods are usually things like pasta sauce, and beans, and those two ingredients can make a kicking chili with little effort.

Another great thing to have on hand is rice. I tend to go for Jasmine or brown rice so I can use it when I make a stir fry. A stir fry is also another quick and easy meal for me because I buy frozen vegetables for it. I keep frozen fish fillets on hand as well, because fish takes about 10 minutes to defrost and 20 minutes to bake.

I also like to use my Crock Pot a lot. Making meals in there is easy for me because it cuts down on the time I have to stand over a stove and I also don't have to constantly get up to look inside the stove to see if the meal is done. Both of which have tired me out on bad days. There are plenty of recipes you can find on the net for the slow cooker, but a general rule of thumb is to add an hour for every 20-30 minutes something needs to be cooked for.

Good food shouldn't have to be complicated, especially when you have Fibromyalgia. I have a few recipes in my first book, *The Fibro Hand*, and they are pretty good, but I'd love to share my vegetarian chili recipe with all of you today.

What you will need:

*2, 20 oz cans of red kidney beans

*1, 26 oz jar of pasta or marinara sauce

1 and a half tablespoons of light brown sugar

1 teaspoon of sea salt

*1 half cup of frozen mixed peppers (red, yellow, and green)

And then add 2-3 teaspoons (or to taste) of the following spices

Coriander

Paprika

Basil

Garlic Powder

Onion Powder

Cilantro

Curry

Cumin

*Chili Pepper Sauce

Add ingredients to a medium to large pot. Cook on medium heat, stirring occasionally, until hot (about 15-20 minutes). Serve immediately and enjoy.

*all ingredients named can be found at Trader Joe's, however, you can substitute these products for your own favorites.

Stay Fabulous!

Love and friendship,

Kimberley

Studies are important for the health community. They help us find out how a disease affects an individual, whether or not a medication works well enough to be placed into mainstream society, what certain environmental effects do to individuals, and if vaccines will work for mainstream society. I have nothing against studies. They are vital in today's society, but I do have something against individuals and drug companies who test medications and vaccines only to a point, and then unleash this stuff onto an unsuspecting society to see the major effects.

Don't get me wrong, tests should constantly be done until the probabilities of something being safe out way the probabilities of it not. However, I get a little nervous when I hear that post-marketing studies will be done to track any cases of autoimmune diseases and musculoskeletal conditions like multiple sclerosis and fibromyalgia on the new FDA backed vaccine Cervarix. You can read about this article on Web MD at http://www.webmd.com/sexual-conditions/hpv-genital-warts/news/20090909/fda-panel-backs-new-hpv-vaccine-cervarix.

The clinical trials did not show that Cervarix can cause any of these diseases, but the FDA wants them to track it-- just in case. Just in case? What worries me is why they have chosen these particular diseases out of all the other diseases out there. Why fibromyalgia, arthritis, and multiple sclerosis? Could it be because of the controversy that Gaurdasil has gotten within recent news in 2009?

Cinda Crawford, host of the **Health Matters** Show, discussed this very topic during her March 13, 2009 show. She states that some studies have shown teenage girls contracting Chronic Fatigue like symptoms and those were the lucky ones. There have been teenagers that died after taking the vaccine. I was alarmed and shocked when I read her posts about this, so shocked, that I wrote into her show about the dilemma I am faced with. My oldest turns 9 this year, and that means she is ready for this vaccine.

Cinda's show was not the only one to report these findings. The *Today* show also did a report on Gaurdasil on August 18, 2009, but the *Today* show did not go into great detail as to what adverse effects were found in teens that took the shot. The article did, however, say that about 6.2 percent of the girls who took the shot experienced serious effects and that 32 deaths had been reported. You can read the report here at,

http://today.msnbc.msn.com/id/32466274/ns/health-cancer/

In my opinion, these three reports make me very nervous about allowing my daughter to even get the vaccine. We have no history of cervical cancer in our family, but we obviously have Fibromyalgia in it. I truly hope more tests are done on **both** of these vaccines so I am more informed on making a good decision for my daughters.

Stay Fabulous

Love and friendship,

Kimberley

Wednesday, November 19, 2008

Soaking Up on Some Knowledge

My Mother got a teaching job when I was little and she'd have me stay with my Grandmother until she came home from work. My Grandmother and I used to have so much fun cooking, making noodles with her noodle maker, cleaning, and just plain talking.

She has always been a great influence in my life and I discuss her and some of her recipes in my book *The Fibro Hand* in better detail. But one of the things she taught me was how to use Epsom Salt to my advantage, the topic for today.

If I had a sprain or strained muscle from gym class or exercise, she'd tell me to soak in Epsom Salt. She'd also use it very often for her feet. She suffered from polio when she was two years old and has post-polio as an adult now. Soaking helps her with inflammation. I remembered this wonderful bit of information when I was surfing the net and I came across one of many social networking sites for Fibromites.

As a side, I think forums and sites that help Fibro sufferers feel like they are not alone are really good for the soul. I suggest looking into them and becoming a member of at least one of them. I run a couple of them myself and you can check them out on my website.

Anyway, getting back to the surfing, one of the members had a question about Epsom Salt helping Chronic Fatigue sufferers. I'd never heard of it helping, but being the type of person I am, I started to surf the net to find out.

The beautiful thing about searching the net is that you can come across a lot of cool info in the process and when I do, I love to pass it on to you, my readers. Well, upon my search, I found a site called Epsom Salt Industry Council. And as you can imagine, they really like the stuff.

What I found was surprising, Epsom Salt's two main components, Magnesium and Sulfate, work wonders in your garden, beauty regimen, and also your health.

The benefits that magnesium has for your health are:

- It can help relieve stress
- Improve your sleep
- Improve your concentration
- Help your nerves and muscles function properly
- Aid in preventing the hardening of arteries and blood clots
- Makes insulin perform better in the body
- Elevates swelling from joints to reduce pain and muscle cramps

- Improves the use of oxygen

The benefits of sulfates are:

- They flush toxins
- Improve your nutrients absorption
- Eases the pain of migraines
- Helps in forming joint proteins, brain tissue, and mucin proteins.

When reading this, I said *hot digity* to myself because it sounds like a great thing for people that suffer from Chronic Fatigue and Fibromyalgia! I'm so glad I decided to soak up some knowledge so I can feel more fabulous. Move over *Victoria's Secret* there's a new relaxation technique in town lol!

Hope you all can give this a try.

Stay Fabulous!

Love and friendship,

Kimberley

Intimacy is an important topic to me because everyone every once in a while needs to physically feel love, not just express it verbally. I've discussed communication in my prior blogs about sex, as well as, the mantra, *It's all about me.* I talk about this subject a lot because it's one that's very near and dear to my husband and myself. Okay, maybe my husband, more, but all kidding aside, this is a huge topic for Fibromyalgia sufferers.

A forum called *Daily Strength* touches on this subject to. You can read the thread here, http://www.dailystrength.org/c/Fibromyalgia/forum/7945901-fibro-sex. The forum goes into great detail as to what works for some and what doesn't. Most have blamed medication as the main culprits for *not* having sex, but for some, it's fear of a flare.

Fear is a funny thing. It can sometimes lead us in the wrong direction in our lives when we feel stuck. I have felt that feeling many times in my own life and have seen it in others on the many fibro forums.

There are so many people that are afraid to have sex because they are afraid of what they will feel like in the morning. That is heartbreaking to me and that is why I decided to write my book, *Fibromyalgia and Sex Can Be a Pain in the Neck...* That book discussed a lot of the basics, like keeping a journal, opening the lines of communication, diet, and getting rid of your guilt.

I really didn't get into the nitty gritty and discuss what works for us. The reason behind leaving that out was purely simply, I didn't want to make the book sound like our positions, techniques, and ways were the know all and be all for Fibro sufferers.

Perhaps I was over analyzing the subject. I tend to do that at times and forget to just go with it. I may have, dare I say, been a bit fearful of what people might have thought about the book too.

Fear is definitely a funny thing that can be detrimental, even in book form. The next time you are overcome with it due to the topic of sex, try to relax a bit. Soak in the tub with the honey and go with the flow. Sometimes a bath or a shower can limber your joints and mood. If you need to, try some Epsom Salt, which helps relieve aching joints, fatigue, and mood. The best part about the salt is that hubby won't have to smell fruity-- a bonus to the masculine man.

As a side note to all of my readers, I am working on a sequel to my *Fibro and Sex* book. It will be a joint effort on my husband's and my part and it will read like a *he said/she said* book. This book is still in its infancy and won't be out for quite some time, but I will keep you updated on its status on my website at http://www.kimberleylinstruth-beckom.com.

Stay Fabulous

Love and friendship,

Kimberley

Monday, December 1, 2008

<u>We May Not Be Right...But At Least We Aren't Wrong</u>

While I was doing a bit of web surfing for a new book I'm researching, I came across a very interesting article that I must share with all of you. The article, which reads more like a press release, is entitled <u>*Fibromyalgia Can No Longer Be Called the 'Invisble' Sydrome?*</u>

The article was released on November 3, 2008 by SNM, Advancing Molecular Imaging and Therapy. From what I can gather, SNM is an organization that is both medical and scientific. The facility wants to spread awareness of what molecular imaging is and how it can help provide good health care for its patients.

The basic premise to the entire article is that through brain scans of 20 Fibromyalgia patients and 10 Healthy women, they have found brain abnormalities in the women who suffer from Fibromyalgia.

So what does this mean for all of us that have suffered with Fibromyalgia? Well, first off, it means that a doctor can't go around telling you that it is *all in your head* or the classic *you're not right*. We who suffer from this beast know that we are not right and that's why we went to a doctor in the first place.

And the reason why they can't just blame it on craziness or depression is because this study clearly showed that anxiety and depression are only symptoms and not the one something that is wrong with us. In other words, anxiety and depression are independent from the abnormalities that they found.

They also found that the Fibromyalgia patients had larger amounts of perfusion in the area of the brain that should discriminate the intensity of pain, and found smaller amounts of perfusion in the part of the brain that is thought to be involved in the emotional response to pain.

So what does this mean in English? We respond to pain differently than *normal* people. That is not a surprise. But what is a surprise, is that they can now see it on SPECT scans of the brain. That means that this study can reinforce the idea that Fibromyalgia is a real disease with honest to goodness proof.

SPECT scans have also been used in studies of chronic fatigue sufferers. Brigham and Women's Hospital and Harvard Medical School have published their SPECT brain scans of chronic fatigue sufferers.

This is a good sign of the times. It shows that people are researching these two diseases that are so very real. It will be interesting to see if they continue to find a correlation between Chronic Fatigue and Fibromyalgia. Some doctors believe that both are one in the same disease.

Either way, we sufferers now know that even though *we may not be right, we at least know we aren't wrong.* And that's *fabulous!*

Stay Fabulous!
Love and friendship,

Kimberley

Fibro and Fabulous

This article appeared in today's health news and it's an exciting find.
http://www.reuters.com/article/healthNews/idUST
RE58L40T20090922?feedType=RSS&feedName=
healthNews

This is yet another study being done on Fibromyalgia's neurological effects on the brain. This study seems a bit more extensive than the previous one I discussed.

166 Fibro sufferers were in this study and 66 were in the control group. Those are fairly high numbers to have for a study. Most studies I have come across for this debilitating disease are very small ones. The groups are of about 20 or so patients along with the control group. To me, this looks promising that more money will be spent on finding a cause and a cure. Since the numbers of sufferers has skyrocketed to about 2-4 percent of the human population, it's important to find out what's going on.

Dr. Nathaniel F. Watson, of the University of Washington Medicine Sleep Institute at Harborview, Seattle, performed the study. He does not want to go out on a limb and say that this study is conclusive, or even promising, but it is a step in the right direction.

With 27 out of 29 neurological categories tested, and with more neurological symptoms being found in the Fibro group, he stresses that neurological examinations need to be performed on patients suffering from Fibromyalgia. With this finding and recommendation, I think we will see a more conclusive and definitive test for Fibromyalgia in the coming years.

Stay Fabulous!

Love and friendship,

Kimberley

In a few previous blog entries, I've discussed the new research going on with Fibromyalgia. This article is yet another showing that the brain is affected.

http://www.sciencedaily.com/releases/2008/03/0803 10112658.htm

What is extremely interesting about this one is the fact that they think glutamate, a brain molecule, is the problem that causes Fibromyalgia. Apparently, if levels are low, pain is decreased. I was thoroughly interested in this article for a very particular reason. I wanted to see if the article discussed a link between Monosodium glutamate (MSG) and glutamate levels in the brain. Unfortunately, it did not.

Glutamate.org (http://www.glutamate.org/Index.asp)

Is a website dedicated to the seasoning. It explains the history of the stuff. It also has an interesting article on its home page. The article is about a study done trying to link MSG to allergic reactions and asthma. It explains that the seasoning has been studied for a period of 40 years (since 1968) and the evidence of a link has failed to determine anything.

I'm not so convinced that this stuff doesn't play a big role on our diet. I know that my symptoms heighten when I consume food containing MSG. Perhaps that may be because I have Fibromyalgia, and my levels of glutamate are already too high. There's a good possibility that MSG is harmless if it is consumed in moderation-- at least-- per the research.

That may be all well and good, however, most of today's processed foods contain MSG. It's possible for an unsuspecting person to consume too much of the seasoning, causing the body to overdose. Once the body overdoses, you can see reactions like allergies, fibromyalgia, and asthma. Granted, I'm no doctor or research scientist, but to me this makes a lot of sense.

I think this is why we see so many diseases like Fibromyalgia being diagnosed in people. It may not be the actual food, but how much of it you have. If companies started making things with less chemicals, we might possibly see a decline in disease. Of course, the same could be said about health care, in that, if doctors diagnosed the whole person instead of the disease, we may see less of it.

This is obviously my opinion and I can't diagnose, treat, or cure anything. I've read a lot of authors who agree with me on the issue, however, I'm just an observer at this point. Like you, I'm waiting patiently for someone to find a link between the food we eat and Fibromyalgia.

What I can do is pass on a bit of advice my Grandmother gave me when I was young. I think it fits and is appropriate for this entry... *Everything in moderation, Kim, everything in moderation.*

Stay Fabulous!

Love and friendship,

Kimberley

This article is really no surprise to the sufferer of Fibromyalgia. Most know that they need to get a restful sleep and that diet and exercise is key in warding off the symptoms that cause flares. In fact, it is vital for the sufferer to do these things in order to be able to function.

What is surprising about this article is the fact that it made the New York Times. This paper is well known for only publishing quality stories that have valid information. The Times does not like being wrong or embarrassed when it comes to the validity of their articles-- a little known fact I learned in a college journalism class.

http://health.nytimes.com/ref/health/healthguide/esn-fibromyalgia-know.html

After a quick search of the term Fibromyalgia in The Times Internet database, it appears that this is the first article about the disease ever published by the paper this year. There are other postings, but these are in blog style, not article form. So, if The Times is publishing stories about Fibromyalgia, that's a good sign that this disease is finally being taken seriously. It's a good step in September, 2009 for Fibro sufferers to *make* The Times, long overdue, but a good step.

Stay Fabulous!

Love and friendship,

Kimberley

A local paper in Canada had this to say about massage therapy and how it may now be taxed. http://www.bclocalnews.com/news/63636317.html I have some readers from Canada and this article infuriated me because it does not seem fair that only the massage therapy industry is being taxed due to a technicality.

Americans do not have universal health care at this point and some think it's a good idea to have it so people can afford medical treatments. I am all for some type of universal health care because I simply can't afford to pay for health care anymore unless I go bankrupt, stop eating, and work only for my doctors.

This article seems to show how certain forms of care can be taxed due to loopholes in the system. That might not bode well for any of us who have to seek alternative forms of health care rather than the norm of pill popping.

It's sad to see this happening in a country that truly prides themselves in helping their people out as best as they can. I hope this loophole gets resolved so the cost of massage is not an issue for anyone that needs it.

Stay Fabulous!

Love and friendship,

Kimberley

Fibro and Fabulous

<u>Thursday, December 4, 2008</u>

<u>To Do's</u>

It is funny how you can run into people you knew way back when. I got together with an old friend of mine that I knew in high school and college. We were very good friends back then and did a lot together. She was one friend who knew theme before all of the Fibro madness caught up with me.

We started talking a bit about my issues with Fibromyalgia and the conversation got strange. You see, she started to ask me how different my life is now after diagnoses. I started to tell her that I have to pace myself with how much I do in a day. There are, of course, days that I don't do that, because I will feel really good and hence, I stretch the limit.

She then asked me what I meant by that and I explained that I had this one day where I cleaned my living room and bathroom from top to bottom, then went to my mother-in-laws and raked about three quarters of the leaves in her back yard with her. I, of course, felt the aches and pains of that day for the next three because of my Fibro and did very little around the house. I said to her that most people would probably be able to do much more than just that. They would probably at least be able to finish the yard. I also explained that not being able to do things or finish things makes me feel guilty.

And then, she said something that I didn't expect. She said you know, Kim, for most people, what you did that day is a lot. That got me thinking because she's right. Even on our bad days we do a lot. We all have to get out of bed, get a shower, get dressed, and eat at least a meal or two. That's a lot. Of course, we don't stop there-- even on our bad days-- because some of us have jobs, kids, housework, and a slue of other responsibilities that we do everyday. That's a lot too.

So with my friend's thoughts in mind, maybe we can all look at ourselves and our, to do list, a little bit differently...

Maybe the best thing that all of us can do for ourselves is to start to celebrate how much we've accomplished so far in the day, or even our lives. Constantly harping on how little of a dent we have made on our always and ever-growing list of things to do, is too negative. When you get right down to it, it's just not what a *fabulous* person would do.

Stay Fabulous!
Love and friendship,

Kimberley

Monday, December 15, 2008

The Holidays And You, Everyday

Let's face it, the holidays are overwhelming at times for us all and saying that they are just stressful can sound like an understatement. When you add a chronic condition to the mix, it can be downright mind blowing for the sufferer.

My family, though lovable, tends to ask me to do things for them at the last possible minute throughout the year, but when it happens to be around this time of year, it just seems worse. For instance, there are many people who like to do cookie exchanges around now, and you usually have to bake at the very least, 5 dozen for those exchanges. There's also the school time fun of Thanksgiving feasts, Christmas gifts for the classroom, cookie treats, school plays and concerts that require outfits, and sometime in between all of this, you are supposed to squeeze in Christmas shopping, and preparing a meal for the whole clan. I don't know about you, but just typing out all of this is making me tired.

So how do you cope? Well, I learned this wonderful word in the English language that seems to work well-- at least some of the time. That beautiful word is the word *no*. Now, it may sound mean to say that kind of word during this very special time of year, but it's really not.

I know that this time of year, we all tend to think about people less fortunate, and of course, all of our friends and loved ones that have helped us in one way or another throughout the entire year. But you also have to think of yourself. You've helped out people this year and you have probably thought about people less fortunate than yourself during the year too. So why beat yourself up for not being able to do it all? During this time of year, especially, you are cramming a year's worth of time into a month.

My grandmother taught me two very important phrases. One is *Christmas is everyday* and the other is *Charity begins at home*. These two phrases are beautiful because they are packed with so much meaning.

Christmas can truly be everyday when you get together with someone you love. Even just calling someone you care about that might be far away is also like a Christmas get together because you are spending time with them.

Charity can't happen unless a person is well enough to give of themselves. So if you are stretching yourself so thin that you may wind up with a flare that lasts all winter long, what good have you truly done if you can't give to yourself or your family? The unfortunate part about having Fibromyalgia is that we have to learn how to manage our time and our pain. Once we learn this valuable lesson, we can be charitable to our family AND to others.

Staying as flare free as possible makes this season extra special because you won't be too tired to see those little ones open up the gifts that Santa gave them. Or bake tons of Christmas cookies with your children to enjoy with their class and Santa of course. Being as flare free as possible might even be enjoyable for those Christmas parties with your partner that require a certain amount of dancing too. So give the word *no* a try with the things that are not as important during this month and have a *fabulous* holiday season!

Stay Fabulous!
Love and friendship,

Kimberley

Fibro and Fabulous

There is a new ad circulating around the air waves of the Internet and the TV for October, 2009. It's an ad campaign against a tax on soda and juices. Some will say that these beverages are a simple luxury that all Americans should enjoy, while others are making it seem like a tax on these products will make it harder for the average American family to be able to put food on the table. One of them can be seen here.

http://www.youtube.com/watch?v=0zmDwMNaTzA

Um, excuse me, but this is just down, right ridiculous. I'm getting tired of these big businesses spending a crap load of our money on commercials that cloud a person's perception into thinking that there is any validity to what is being said.

The commercial that takes the cake (pardon the sweet pun here) is the one with the woman who is upset because juices and soda will be taxed. Well, either this woman actress is clearly misinformed as to what a well balanced diet should contain, or the ad was made to purposely fool us into thinking our Juicy Juice, Apple and Eve, Welch's, and other 100% real juices are going to be taxed. The commercial I'm referring to can be seen here.

http://www.youtube.com/watch?v=sxIwwrO2JYg

This is so far from the truth, it is really not funny. Only sugary beverage drinks that are not real juice and contain high fructose corn syrup will be taxed. I'm sure the people that funded the ads saying that high fructose corn syrup is "made from real corn and is okay in moderation" are the ones funding this silly campaign.

Regardless of whether they are or not, I sure hope no one is duped into thinking that this is a bad thing. I have always been an advocate for eating healthy. It's a rare occasion for us to have any type of sugared drink in our home. We don't do it often because we are trying to eat healthy, and frankly, we need to pinch our pennies like everyone else.

What's ironic is that this commercial is a lot like the statement that made Marie Antoinette famous, "Then let them eat cake."

If you truly are poor and are pinching your pennies, sugar is not an option because you can't afford it. Maybe these people funding the commercial should go back to school for a bit and relearn economics.

I know there is question as to whether or not the story of Marie Antoinette is really true. Some believe that those words were never uttered. I think that big business should learn the story anyway. It would show them just how silly they really are.

Stay Fabulous!

Love and friendship,

Kimberley

Friday, December 26, 2008

<u>Care giving</u>

Care giving is one of the hardest jobs out there. We have caregivers for many diseases and disorders. Some of these care givers are from the health professional industry and some are friends and family. It can be a thankless job for these people because they feel misunderstood.

They can get frustrated because they may not know how to help the person they are caring for. They also tend to try and remain strong and tough. They act like nothing can hurt them-- no matter what you throw their way. Of course, this can be so far from the truth.

As a mom, I can relate to care giving when I tend to my children. My youngest is just under a year old and her only form of communication is crying, so it can be hard sometimes to figure out what has gotten her upset since she can't use words to communicate. It's also hard when you try to help, like feed her or change her diaper, only to find out that she's sick with a cold, or has gas. You feel helpless because you know that all you can do is just be there and hold her hand through the ordeal.

As a daughter to a Mom with Alzheimer's, I can relate to care giving for an adult who finds it hard to communicate. At times, this can be extremely frustrating for both the patient and the caregiver because an adult feels like they should be able to tell you what's wrong. The care giver can feel helpless in this situation because communicating may be futile with a person that might not understand what you are saying.

From time to time in my own life, I to need the help of a care giver because of the health issues I have. This is hard for me because I've always been very independent and I feel that if I can't do something, I should not be burdening someone else to do it for me. So I can understand the patient's side of the coin as far as frustration is concerned. They're frustrated, however, for a different reason.

Most people don't want help for something simple, like opening up a jar. Some people can even feel embarrassed when they need help with things like buttoning a shirt or combing one's hair. I know I've felt silly when I've had to ask my husband to help me with taking off my shoes because I couldn't bend down to do it myself. It can make one feel inadequate as a human being because these are some normal functions that people take for granted every day.

So how does one try to maintain feeling fabulous when their body isn't working like it should? Well, I find that there isn't just one answer to this question, but many. This, of course, is from being able to understand both sides of the coin, as well as, listening to my care giver when he talks to me about doing things out of love.

I can't stress enough how important it is to communicate to your loved ones how you feel. They won't be able to truly understand you or what you go through unless you do. Sometimes you may feel like a broken record because you'll have to repeat yourself-- a lot. But it's worth it because they love you, and they can't love you completely unless they know the whole you.

The same can be said about us trying to understand them and what they go through when we give them a hard time about helping us. The care giver should also be trying to communicate with you too so you can love them as completely as you can.

Another thing that helps me is being able to step back from the situation itself and try and remember that it's just a situation that is allowing me to be able to grow in love and understanding. This is hard when I feel silly asking my husband to help me get up from the floor-- or my particular favorite-- helping me to straighten out my back so I can stand up straight after doing heavy housework. But it can work.

The last thing that I try to remember is that tomorrow is another day. Another day, that can, and usually does bring something better. A day that is a little less painful. And one where I can tie my own shoes and pop the emergency brake lever on my own. Being able to step back and think this way allows me to feel fabulous. I hope it helps you feel fabulous too.

Stay Fabulous!
Love and friendship,

Kimberley

Health care reform needs to be done. There is no way we Americans can put this off any longer. As a nation, we have been talking about reform since FDR was president. That's too long of a time to be in just the talking stages.

Some of you may wonder which side of the fence I reside on due to my opinions. The truth is, I have no idea. I didn't even know parties could swing left or right until I heard a conversation earlier this year. In my family, I was raised republican and taught to vote republican, but as an adult, I don't always vote republican. I vote for whom I think is best. If that makes me a *left*, a *right*, or somewhere in between, so be it. I don't consider myself affiliated with any party and that includes independents.

What I strongly agree with is the fact that we as Americans need to do something about health care so it is more affordable for everyone living here. It should be a God given right to be healthy. We shouldn't have to decide between paying for our health or our food. What I find appalling is the fact that people in the House and Senate want to continue to sit on this important issue. I'm sorry, but doing something is really a lot better than doing nothing. They have a job that allows them cushy health care benefits. Most Americans are not so lucky.

Fibro and Fabulous

Earlier this year, I wrote to President Obama and let him know about my health care story. I explained that my health care is so expensive that our family has had to put our dreams of owning a home on the back burner. We have had so many problems trying to stay afloat with the bills that we have not been able to afford a home for about 10 years now. When you are sick, you shouldn't have to worry about the cost.

It is a known fact that Americans are either an illness or a job loss away from bankruptcy. Those are pretty scary statistics. Costs have gotten so out of control that stress is building up in the sick. When stress levels run high, most people become sicker, not better. It's no wonder we are in a crisis today. My story was posted on the national health care support site among many others to show everyone just how devastating an illness can be.

Another story made it to a South Carolina's editorial page and was posted today, October 7, 2009. You can read the story here.

http://www2.scnow.com/scp/news/opinion/letters_to
_the_editor/article/letter_to_the_editor_presidents_h
ealth_care_plan_needs_to_be_supported/79666/

It is bad enough that people are losing their jobs due to the economy. No one should have to experience job loss because they can't afford to feel better.

Stay Fabulous!

Love and friendship,

Kimberley

Tuesday, January 6, 2009

Out With The Old

New Years is a great time to think about what you want to accomplish for the year. Everyone seems to get that fresh motivation and resolve to do something for themselves to make things healthier, easier, or just plain better. When I was a teen, I used to spend my New Years Eve listening to Casey's countdown. I would pull out my journal and read through all the things that happened to me over the year and then I'd figure out what I'd want to do better and what (or who) I'd want to leave alone for the new year.

Once I got older and had children, I stopped that tradition I had for myself. A young child and reading anything with words don't mix well. Writing was sheer torture too. There were days when trying to write out the shopping list was next to impossible. But when I look back on it all, it was really something I should have never stopped doing.

Having an illness like Fibromyalgia can get you down sometimes. It's not an easy thing to have because there really are days when you just don't feel like getting out of bed. But you do, you get out of bed and you start your day. It's something that should make you proud because it's an accomplishment on those bad days. I always seem to forget that, though. I'm always feeling guilty that I can't do more. I even feel bad when I cancel plans on a bad day.

I really shouldn't feel bad, though, since there are days when I feel like I'm on top of the world and I can clean my house, my mother in-law's yard, and help out my own mother with cleaning too--all in the same day. So really, those days make up for my bad ones.

You are probably wondering what this all has to do with New Years, huh? Well, plenty, if you start to incorporate your reflections of the New Year with your good days of being pain-free. In other words, the next time you have a good day, write down everything you did and how it felt when you did it. Add the date if you want so you can start to track your good months too. But the main purpose of this journal will be for reflection only.

Then, the next time you have one of those bad days, take out that journal and start to read it. I bet you will be amazed at how much you can do. It will hopeful kill any of those old negative, guilty feelings you may have when you can't do something on your bad days. And that would be fabulous!

Happy New Year

Stay Fabulous!
Love and Friendship,

Kimberley

Fibro and Fabulous

Thursday, January 22, 2009

The Competition Expands Along With My Thoughts

Cymbalta and Lyrica, FDA approved drugs for Fibromyalgia patients, now have some more competition. A new drug was just approved this month for the treatment of Fibromyalgia. Savella, (milnacipran) is another antidepressant drug that is officially out on the market for Fibro sufferers in the US.

This drug is a bit different than other antidepressant drugs because it boosts levels of norepinephrine more so than levels of serotonin. This drug has been used in over 50 countries for the past 10 years for the treatment of depression. The drug's side effects are mild.

The drug is only approved for adults at this point and not for children, since it is an antidepressant. However, the FDA wants some post marketing studies done on women who are pregnant and breastfeeding while taking Savella. This is wonderful news. There are very little drugs that pregnant Fibro patients can use, so anything that has been proven relatively safe for this group is pretty welcome.

There are other drugs that are still being tested for treatment of Fibromyalgia and it is unclear as to when they will be approved. One in particular will be applying for a New Drug Application later on this year. This drug is called JZP-6 (sodium oxybate) and is being used by some patients now. The FDA may make a decision on this drug by 2010 or 2011.

One can only hope that this may mean research into other treatments, including alternative treatments, for this debilitating syndrome. Research was done in 2006 on an Eastern form of treatment known as acupuncture. This research found that acupuncture did help patients who suffered from Fibro.

This form of treatment that inserts needles in certain areas of the body using heat or electrical stimulation, is used as a way of allowing the body to naturally heal from disease, disorders, or injuries. It's been used to relieve things like PMS, migraines, and even Fibromyalgia.

The Today Show did an alternative health segment on acupuncture this morning, and that may spark popularity in this treatment again. Even some insurance companies have warmed up to acupuncture and are allowing patients to get this treatment through their health care plan.

The possibilities of treatment for a once named controversial syndrome are expanding and this news makes me feel fabulous! Hope you are fabulous too!

Stay Fabulous!
Love and friendship,

Kimberley

Wednesday, January 28, 2009

Excercise Shouldn't Cost You An Arm or a Leg

In today's world, everything costs money, and with money being tight for everyone due to the recession, money spent on frills is getting cut out of the budget. I'm not a one to have many frills in my life because frankly, I just simply could never afford them-- even when things were good. I'm the type of person that spends on everyone else but myself. My only exception to this rule is when it comes to my health. That's today's blog topic.

You see, I feel that everyone is entitled to spend some money on themselves when it comes to being healthy on a day-to-day basis. After all, real food, not that fake stuff, costs money.

Exercising costs money too. But as far as exercising is concerned, I feel that it should not cost you an arm and a leg every time you feel like going to the gym. The only thing you should be losing is weight, not money.

I don't go to the gym or even take a yoga class. That's right, you heard me-- I don't go out to exercise. I stay in to get my work out. I probably burn just as many calories at home as I would out in a gym-- maybe even more. What do I do at home? What's my secret?

I practice my yoga at home by popping in a video 1-2 times a week. I love how convenient this is too because I don't have to rush out the door (and bring my blood pressure to a boil) to make a 10 AM class.

It's also better for me because I'm the type of person who gives into peer pressure. I know, call me crazy and a bit childish, I should have left that awkward stage of peer pressure back in high school when I graduated, but I didn't. If someone out there, like an instructor, wants me to turn my body into a pretzel, I'm trying to do it. I know I'm going to regret that move tomorrow when I can't get out of bed. Yet, I still do it.

With a video in, and no one watching, no one will ever know that I fast forward the parts that I can't do. If I can't stand on my head, no one needs to know. Yoga is about stretching one's limits-- not breaking them. If I can't do it, I gently get out of the move and wait for the next.

Another thing I love to do is gardening. I'm an HGTV freak and I love *The Garden Guy* on *Gardening by the Yard*. He's a little wacky, yeah, but I am too. Anyways, on one episode they were discussing how gardening is a lot like lifting weights at the gym. Now, I don't lift weights at the gym, but I do garden, so that got my attention.

Fibro and Fabulous

Apparently, the simple motion of shoveling dirt actually mimics what you would do when lifting some weights on a gym set! I think that's awesome because I don't have to pay for a gym membership. I just have to go out in my mother in-law's yard and do some gardening for her when I want a work out. Of course, there's even more of a bonus when you garden because if you plant vegetables like me, you don't have to buy them at the supermarket either!

Okay, by now you are probably thinking that I NEVER leave my house. Well, that's not true. I don't live with my mother in-law, so I do have to drive to her house to garden. But all kidding aside, I do get out and actually drive somewhere at least once a week with my daughters in tow.

Where do we go? We go out to get some exercise by walking the malls. Now, if you are a shop-a-holic, I wouldn't recommend this one, but if you are a tight wad like me-- go have some fun browsing! It can't hurt to just look and you can get plenty of exercising walking around from shop to shop. I've put on a pedometer on some shopping excursion and found that I walked the equivalent of 4 miles in one trip. That was a lot of steps, and a few too many hours at the mall (about 3), so if you don't like the mall that much-- go for a mile which turns out to be close to an hour's worth of steps.

There's lots of ways to exercise without spending a lot at a gym. These are just a couple of ways to stay fabulous and feel fabulous. There, of course, are many more, but those will be for another blog.

Stay Fabulous!
Love and friendship,

Kimberley

This article is just plain funny. I remember when this first study came out stating that women were less tolerant to pain than men. Any woman who has spent a considerable amount of time with a man knows that men do not handle pain well. They tend to complain about it more and it bothers them for much longer than a woman. Having the flu can seem like a death sentence to some men because they are incredibly uncomfortable.

http://abcnews.go.com/Health/WireStory?id=871272 6&page=1

I know there were many times when I was pretty sick, at least, according to my doctor, and I felt very little discomfort. I personally was more annoyed than anything else. So I truly found the research comical.

What is great about this recent research is that they are now finding that women can endure pain for longer periods. Of course, any woman who has given birth could have told them that-- but at least they have documentation backing that statement up. It's sad that they had to spend a ton of money on a study that seems like a no-brainer, but there is a positive side to this, I guess. The positive outcome is that it is paving the way for more studies on women and pain receptors.

Stay Fabulous!

Love and friendship,

Kimberley

Thursday, February 5, 2009

Space Invaders in the Bedroom

I'm going to go into a topic that's a bit near and dear to me since I have little ones. The topic today is co-sleeping, or what I like to term as *space invaders in the bedroom*. Babies can take up a lot of room in your house and sometimes they can take over your room-- your bedroom that is. It can put a damper on what little sex life you may have left with your partner and it can even try your patience.

Co-sleeping is a controversial topic with mothers, fathers, doctors, and the like, but it is something that parents will inevitably deal with from to time whether they believe in it or not. Let's face it-- kids get sick and want their parents, the air conditioner may only reach so far, there's a bad thunderstorm and your bedroom is a safer place, your child has a nightmare, and the list can go on and on as to why your child may need to spend the night in mommy and daddy's room.

For a mother who suffers from Fibromyalgia, getting up to answer a newborn baby's cries can be difficult, and at times, can seem down, right impossible. Having fibro means not sleeping well to begin with, and when you add a newborn into the mix, you probably will be lucky to get a solid two hours a night. Getting out of bed can be a feat at times due to stiffness when you deal with this condition, as well, so what does a mom do when faced with this night after night?

The answer I came up with is simple... anything that works!

When I was pregnant with my first daughter, Brittanny, I wound up doing everything opposite of what the experts tell you to do. I ate McDonald's when I felt like it, I cleaned out the cat box, I also got my nails done once, and yes, I even decided to bottle feed my first daughter because I was going to have to go right back to work after 6 weeks.

I was young, very naive, and had no time to read up on what the experts were saying because I was working my tail off to pay up on my college debt. But, those were the days, I tell you, because I could be up all day and all night. I was also pain free during those first few years that my daughter was a newborn and toddler.

It wasn't until my daughter turned three, that I started to show serious signs of fibromyalgia pain. Before diagnoses, having a second child was not even a thought, let alone a possibility. But after I knew what I had, I thought things might be a little easier once I knew my limitations.

One of those limitations was getting up in the middle of the night, and since my husband worked many different hours, day and night being a truck driver, I knew this limitation had to be solved on my own. I started to try and find an answer by researching everything I could on mothers of newborns who have fibromyalgia.

I obviously couldn't find much since fibromyalgia is still considered a new disorder, so I started with the next best thing, I researched mothers with a chronic condition. I found mothers who were diabetic, mothers with cancer, and mothers with rheumatoid arthritis, just to name a few.

These mothers' stories were inspiring and informative and even though each one of them had different diseases they were dealing with, they all had one thing in common-- each one of them decided to breast feed their baby. I was astonished at that discovery because frankly, I didn't think it would have been possible for them to even think about breast feeding their baby because of their illness, and yet, they were.

This got me intrigued to learn more, to say the least, so I started to research mothers with illness and breast feeding. The first site that popped up on the net was La Leche League and I found that they not only had information for mothers who suffer from fibromyalgia, but a forum that had mothers helping mothers too! This was an awe inspiring moment for me because I then realized that a second baby could actually be possible.

I knew that pregnancy and after birth may be difficult with fibromyalgia, since my medication was out of the question, but I wanted to have another child, and I figured that if a gal with cancer or arthritis could do it, so could I.

Before I was four months along in my pregnancy with Olivia, I decided that breast feeding might be the best option for me because I wouldn't have to get up and make a bottle-- that step would be eliminated. Researching a little further, I also found out that breast feeding might even be beneficial because serotonin is released in the body-- something that can help a fibro suffer who has trouble sleeping.

Now, of course, breast feeding is good for the baby, but I'm not going to go into any of that here for two reasons, one, this is a blog about Fibromyalgia, and two, I'm not one of those mothers that insists you need to breast feed your child for x amount of reasons because it's the only way to feed your baby. I'm sure any mother reading this *knows* one of those kinds of mothers and that's not my intention-- or even the point of this blog entry.

Now that that's out of the way, let's continue with the co-sleeping idea. I was hemming and hawing on this idea because I really didn't want a child to be sleeping next to me. Don't get me wrong-- I love my kids and I'd do anything for them-- unless it interferes with my ability to take care of them.

Co-sleeping can have that affect if you or your child are light sleepers, can't stay on one side of the bed, or even snore. It can also be a negative if your child would rather sleep with you instead of their own bed too.

But one of the positives is that when your little one is crying to be nursed, you just have to turn to her to do so. That's a plus because you can get the sleep you need while satisfying your baby's needs in the process.

This is something my husband and I decided to try so it would be easier on me when I had to get up. We moved our furniture in our bedroom around a bit and rolled a portable bassinet into the room. Whenever Olivia needed to feed, all I had to do was reach into her bassinet.

Once Olivia got a bit older (and a bit heavier), we decided to have her in the bed with us so I didn't have to lift her at night. This worked out fabulously and little Olivia was very content. So, if you plan on having a child, give co-sleeping a try for a night or two-- it can't hurt and the benefits might just be fabulous for you too!

Stay Fabulous!
Love and friendship,

Kimberley

Sleep is very important to Fibro sufferers. It is very hard for us to get the kind of restful sleep that we may need. I have come across many, many articles about sleep, but nothing that had extensive research. I also never found one that had a lot of good tips.

Sure there's the typical, set a sleep schedule, but what someone should do to relax before bed, varies greatly. Some suggest that reading a book before bed is okay, others don't. Some say that TV and other electronics should be avoided one hour before bed, while others insist it should be a minimum of two. The information can get very confusing.

Below is an article that I find particularly helpful. I think it has practical advice for someone who is truly having problems sleeping. I don't know about you, but I tend to lie in bed wide awake for hours at times. I become nervous about the morning because I know I need to wake up to get the kids ready, and yet, I can't sleep a wink some nights. I now know that it is okay to get up when this happens.

http://www.gulfnews.com/nation/Health/10349940.html

Stay Fabulous!

Love and friendship,

Kimberley

Tuesday, February 24, 2009

<u>Why "Going Green" May Make You See Red</u>

We all know that our planet isn't in the best of shape and each and every one of us is trying to help save our environment in any way that we can. Some of us are making our homes more energy efficient, some of us are bringing our own bags at shopping centers, others of us are choosing eco-friendly cleaning products, and some are looking to make animals' lives a little better.

For some, *going green* also means making better choices in our food consumption too. Foods that are filled with hormones, fillers, additives, chemicals, and pesticides are not only bad for the environment, they're bad for our bodies in some cases. People may have food allergies or sensitivities to certain chemicals, and in some instances, have even built up an intolerance to an additive. I know this to be true since I have fibromyalgia and I have sensitivities.

Whatever the reasons may be for *going green*, it's still a good idea to do as much as you can because some research is showing that certain things really are making a difference. Even something as small as allowing chickens to roam free on the farm can produce better quality eggs and this is something that has gotten attention. But *exactly* what kind of attention may be left up to the eye of the beholder.

Fibro and Fabulous

An interesting article entitled, *Reality Check*, has come out in this month's issue of **The Oprah Magazine** that states that *free range* or *free roaming* chicken product labels may only mean that a chicken has access to the outside for a certain amount of time each day. In other words, a chicken coop door could be open for five minutes every day, and that would constitute a manufacturer being allowed to slap a *free range* label on their product.

The article also mentions that you can look up any green label at *Consumer Reports'* Greener Choices Eco-labels (greenerchoices.org/eco-labels), but being the savvy kind of gal I am, I decided to take a look at it for myself and give you an opinion about the whole thing...

Words on products like, *No steroids, antibiotics, hormones, or additives,* are only claims that the manufacturer has put on a product. These claims have not been certified by an outside third party. Okay, you might say, I know that people selling products can claim anything and the buyer should beware, but did you know that eggs contain more labels on them than any other product out there? And did you know that the USDA has not made any kind of standards for organic fish products?

Gluten-free products may not be truly free of gluten either. In fact, any product that has less than 200 parts per million (ppm) of gluten after finalization, can be considered gluten-free. Why is this you may ask? Well, according to the U K's Food Standards Agency, it would be impossible to remove every spec of gluten from a product, hence, there are standards.

The nice part about this, though, is that the FDA (as of August 2008) wants to make an international standard of 20 ppm for all products. The sweeter deal? If you happen to find a label on food from *The Gluten-Free Certification Organization,* a group that is part of the Gluten Intolerance Group, you can be rest assured that the product contains no more than 10 ppm of gluten.

Kosher products are another product that have labels. They have become famous for high quality, clean products because standards are set higher than the USDA's, but does that also mean that they are vegan friendly? Again, sadly, this may not be the case due to limitations.

According to the Spring 1996 issue of the Jewish Newsletter, Kosher Parve products can contain eggs, honey, and fish due to Jewish law. And products that contain no dairy, may have been produced on machinery that was used for other dairy products. If a machine was not properly boiled, dairy can remain on the metal. This can cause cross-contamination in a sense. So it is best to read the whole label in this case too.

With all of these limitations and regulations, it makes one wonder what you can truly believe. The good news is that some labels from outside sources will certify a product. That's great, and yet, it's a bit scary. What I mean by that is, you've heard the old saying, did you check for the doctor's credentials on the wall (i.e. diploma)? Well, did you ever think you'd see the day where you'd have to check for your food's credentials? I know we get label conscience and all, but don't you think that's a little crazy?

Due to these labels, limiting what we can't eat has gotten real popular today. There are elimination diets and we tend to steer clear of carbs and fried foods if we have high cholesterol. But we all have to eat in order to survive, so what does one really do in this case?

There may not be a real clear-cut answer, but there are some solutions that might fit your lifestyle. Going to a natural food store might free up some of your label-reading time to do other things, like planting a vegetable garden, for instance.

Gardening is fun and it can be as inexpensive and organic as you want it to be. The kids and I have a lot of fun with it and it truly teaches them how to work with what you've got. In fact, you don't even need a back yard if you don't have one. We don't, but we do have pots and soil that are growing some tomatoes, basil, rosemary, lemons, lettuce, and peppers as we speak! We can't wait for the lettuce to fully bloom, but I will tell you that we took a few bites and it's gooooood!

So when you try to *go green* for the environment, try not to get red at those manufactures, curse them, become a hermit, and go on a hunger strike. It's not worth it. Have fun with the whole thing, be creative, that's being *green* whether you realize it or not.

I'll post more about my garden in later blogs. I will try and post a few pictures for you too. Take care for now.

Stay Fabulous!
Love and friendship,

Kimberley

Fibro and Fabulous

Tuesday, March 3, 2009

Calming the Beast

I came across a really funny news story about an hour or two ago and it was interesting enough for me to share. The story is about playing Barry Manilow's music in a strip mall so the teenagers will stay out.

What I found funny was the fact that the teenagers found the music choice to be out of date. I grew up with Barry. I remember the long hair, bell bottoms, and shells he wore while singing *Mandy*. I was just a little thing when *Mandy* came out, but it wasn't *that* long ago!

The thing that isn't funny about the article is the reason why the mall decided to go with easy listening music. They chose it because it can calm one's mind. They figure that the teens won't hang around spray painting their names onto the store fronts if *Can't Smile Without You* is playing.

Now, teens are teens, and I really find it hard to believe that Barry will stop them from coming to the mall. But what may happen is that some of the adults will feel good enough to stay and shop. Supermarkets at one point, did some research into the shopping habits of the female shopper, and found out that their *target shopper* will buy more if easy listening music is played.

Now, that may sound like nonsense, but the facts are true because soft music will calm the beast and help you to relax. I find that my clearest moments are those when relaxing music is on. Granted, I like rock and roll too, and I will put on some 80's Hair Bands when I'm cleaning the house, but when I'm trying to concentrate on a writing piece, I've got Barry on.

Life can be stressful and turn your body and head into knots. Having fibro can make it worse, but if you can find something that will help, like listening to music, it can make things a little more fabulous.

By the way, don't forget about the contest I'm running! Please keep the comments coming, we are almost half way there to giving away the first book.

Stay Fabulous!
Love and friendship,

Kimberley

Thursday, March 5, 2009

<u>Sound Off</u>

Something that never ceases to amaze me is how misunderstood we sufferers can be. It's something that we have all dealt with from time to time, but really, should we have to in today's day and age?

I have always been an advocate of living life to its fullest. I don't think anyone should sit on the sidelines and let wonderful things slip through their grasp just because they are scared, depressed, sick, or just plain feeling stuck in life. Lots of things can be wonderful excuses for us NOT to live our fullest lives, but when you come down to thinking about it, those excuses really are just ways for us to stop trying.

I remember when I was a first semester freshman in college and I got my grades. I was always a good student, but college was different and my grades truly showed that because I did awful. I failed my first semester miserably and I remember feeling like I let everyone down. I even felt guilty that my parents were footing the tuition for a failure. I had a long talk with my mom that night and told her that college wasn't for me and that I'd be better off at a retail job until I could hack the grownup world of college. I told her I didn't want her paying for a failure and that I would work towards my own education and some day go back.

To make an incredibly long story short, my mom was furious with me-- but not because of my grades like I thought she'd be. She was mad that I would give up so easily at something she knew I clearly loved. I started college because I wanted to be a journalist and my mom knew how much I loved to write. Writing has always been a part of me-- even when I was very young, I loved to write. She told me that under no uncertain terms, I'd continue to go to college because she believed in financing my future.

I didn't know what to think, but I went back after break and I looked at college in a different light and applied some different study habits. I went from a 1.5 GPA my first semester, to a 3.0 GPA the second. What's the moral of the story? If I used my *excuses* as a way of quitting college, I would have never gone back and succeeded the way that I did.

My college experience is a lot like my diagnoses of fibromyalgia. I could have given up and stopped doing the things that I enjoy, like yoga, gardening, karaoke, playing with my daughters, heck, even having a second child, the list could go on and on at what I could give up, quit, or stop trying as an *excuse*. But I didn't do that. I still do what I love, just not as often or as long as I used to due to fatigue and pain. I look at the activity in a different way now, just like I did with college.

What ceases to amaze me, though, is that there are still some *Negative Nellies* that think that the pain should run your life and not the you. I've come across many Nellies over the years because I'm a writer, but what is so disheartening isn't what's directed towards me. I write because I feel a need to say something positive, a negative comment isn't going to change the way I think, but it might change someone else's thoughts, and that's the sad part.

Patients with fibromyalgia have been misunderstood for centuries. We don't need anymore negativity in our lives. People who can't see that are just making this beast we deal with even more misunderstood, and that's just sad.

So, the next time you come across *Nellie,* knock her off your friend's list. I know I will.

Stay Fabulous!
Love and friendship,

Kimberley

Thursday, March 12, 2009

<u>Health Care, the Good and the Ugly</u>

This may sound like it's a bit off topic, but hear me out and then you'll know why it applies to fibro. I was listening to NPR and the Today show this morning and found some interesting admissions about the state of the world today on both shows.

Now, I know that listening to the news can be hazardous to my health and cause me a lot of undue stress, but do you know that going to the doctor for "routine" tests could also be hazardous to your health too? The Today show had a topic this morning about the testing for certain cancers. The segment went into saying that even though these screening for cancers can pick up a tumor, a doctor can't tell if the tumor is deadly or not. They also don't know if they are "over treating" the cancer because of this finding.

I must say that I am by no means telling any of you to stop getting physicals or tests that may help save your life, but I am cautioning you as to what I see as something capitalistic.

Doctors are trained to help people, yes, they have taken a medical oath to do so. They are told certain things in medical school, like certain testing will help prevent this or that. But they may have been fed the same load of crap we all have been fed at one point or another in life.

What I mean by this is that by learning, said test, will help, they of course want to use it to do just that for you, just like a certain medicine might help, or a procedure. I have no problem with that, but what I do have a problem with is who is giving them this kind of information.

Are the people making the drug giving truly unbiased clinical trials on their drugs? What about these tests for cancer? Why is there all of the sudden conflicting reports? Could it be that there is something else on the horizon that they want the medical community to believe in and prescribe to patients?

Maybe I might be sounding a bit cynical, but really, how much of what they are feeding us as a truth is really just that, a truth? And how much of it is someone "bending" it to sell their products. When you boil everything down, someone was making money off of these tests and pills, so how bias can they truly be?

NPR was doing a segment on how frugal Americans have been becoming as of late. Americans on average have been saving about 5% of their income since this past December, a number that is surprising because on average, no American has been saving for the past two decades. The special guest was asked how frugal he thought society might take this.

And his answer was surprising, but all too true.

He stated that most people before the fall of economy were interested in "bells and whistles" on products. He used a refrigerator as an example. Most people wanted a water dispenser or maybe if you were lucky enough to afford it, a TV on the gosh darned thing. Now, people want a product to last and are not as concerned about the "look" of it. He went further to say that fridge manufacturers will probably be coming out with things that actually last like they once did.

Now, why is this surprising? Well, if you are like me, you go out and buy something in the hopes that you get some really good use out of it. For instance, I don't buy a car and then turn it in after four years, I actually drive it until it can't be driven anymore. Go ahead, you can call me weird for that statement.

I've had two cars in my 20 years of driving experience. That's on average, 1 every 10 years. The first one I got at 23, 7 years after I first started learning how to drive. The second I got after being without a car for 3 years, and that was 6 years ago. That car is now the only family car we have.

I buy everything with the intention of having it for a long time and I get ticked off when I buy an article of clothing that falls apart or a vacuum that burns out in a manner of a year. I don't have a ton of money to waste on frivolous things and I have even less to buy the good stuff, so we often go without and make do with what we do have because my intention is NOT to waste money.

I can also truly say that I don't do the extras when it comes to my fibro. I can't afford costly medication that will probably wind up killing my liver one day anyway. I also can't afford to go to a rheumatologist once a month so he can "assess" how well I'm doing on medication. I used to feel ashamed about that because the media seems to constantly drill into us that we need to be health conscious and concerned. But I don't feel that way anymore.

Why? Because I truly feel that a lot of this stuff that's out there that is supposed to help us or make things easier on us is just a ploy to get us to spend money, and in some cases, money we don't have. I will still go to the doctor when I need to, but when I do, I am taking more action than I used to.

Before the doctor even starts to draw blood, fill out a script, or whatever it may be, the first things that come out of my mouth are, how much is this going to cost me?, and, what are the side effects? I am passionate about taking care of myself in ALL aspects of my life, not just the problem at hand, so if I've got to stress over the bill, it's just not worth it to me and I will find another way. To me, feeling fabulous, is about achieving an all around general well-balanced approach to life.

Stay Fabulous!
Love and friendship,

Kimberley

Thursday, March 19, 2009

<u>Flares</u>

Flares are a major part of what we deal with when it comes to having Fibromyalgia. They can last anywhere from one day to months depending on what we do or eat. Our body can also sometimes react to the change in temperature.

Most people look forward to the season change, and I admit that I used to too, but since being diagnosed, I look at them with a bit of dread sometimes too. You see, my flares tend to worsen when the temperatures are warm in the day and really cold at night. Twenty degree changes reek havoc on my joints and can make me very tired. There are days when I just want my favorite pair of sweat pants, sweat shirt, turtle neck, and robe, and that's about it. But sometimes, you can't stay in bed. Sometimes you have important things to do like a parent-teacher conference, or you need to go to work.

So how can one feel fabulous on days like these? It's not easy-- I can tell you that much. But there are a few things that get me by on the bad days. One is my kids. The power of love is a strong thing and can be the best medicine around.

My oldest, who is eight, has seen me go through a lot with this beast. There were times that I literally couldn't get up from the couch after an eight hour day of work. But I never wanted to disappoint her when she asked me to play go fish or even run the water for her bath. We would make a game out of getting Mommy up. I'd have her try and pull me up from the couch when she was about 4. I would eventually get up with her *help*. It was fun for her and yet, it gave me some time to alert my body that it was time to move.

When I had my youngest, who just turned 14 months, we considered her our *miracle child*. We had her after we found out I had gotten a handle on my Fibro and knew what my limitations would be. Round the clock feedings were not a picnic, but she kept me going with each smile. The serotonine from breast feeding her helped, as well.

My husband keeps me going too by lending a hand when (or where) I need it. There are days that I just don't know what I'd do without him.

We all have days when the phone rings and we may not want to talk to that person on the other end of the phone. Sometimes they just don't get how tired or achy we may be feeling, but at times it can be us that makes the mistake of shutting them out.

I know I've done it. I had a friend who thought I could cure myself if I'd take certain supplements or go on a certain diet. She would come over and get this twinkle in her eye and take me to places to find a *cure.* I knew I was in trouble, so some days, I just wouldn't answer the phone.

Now, thinking back, maybe I should have, because even though she really didn't understand the research of this disease, she understood that her friend needed her around. This is of course, another great form of medicine, whether we want to admit it to ourselves or not.

I can take my flares for granted sometimes. I see them as me being me and I get alone in my zone of feeling bad. But when somebody rolls down their window at school drop off to make sure I'm okay, or a clerk at a grocery store stops me and asks if I need help getting my groceries in my car, I take notice.

I take notice, give thanks to the person at hand, and then at that point realize that my flare isn't as bad as I thought. It's not as bad because I am realizing at that moment that people really do care-- no matter how big or how small it may be at the time it is assumed.

Take thought in the little things when you can, it may help with your flares. And don't forget about my contest! The 25th commenter will get a free copy of one of my books. That number is coming up soon!

Stay Fabulous!
Love and friendship,

Kimberley

Friday, March 27, 2009

Shopping for ZZZ's

Every so often I get an email from someone who suggests a particular subject matter for my blogs. They usually will contain not only the idea, but a product that they happen to sell and, of course, would love a plug from me. I don't mind these emails too much because I used to work in retail management for eighteen years and I know what it's like to have to sell a quota.

I also know what it's like when a boss wants you to think "outside the box" and surf the Internet for the next way to sell that gem of a product. Selling is a hard job, and at times, customer service is a thankless one too.

The hardest thing today is to try and sell yourself and your product to a perfect stranger via email, because, frankly, most people won't give it a second thought when they hit the Spam button. I do it a lot, however, I'm one of the few people that actually reads the gosh darn thing BEFORE I hit the spam button. Call me crazy, but I take the power of the spam button VERY seriously.

An email sent to me today from a gal by the name of Kirsten, caught my attention, though. It had nothing to do with the actual product, or even her introduction that made this email special, in fact, I've never had a need for her product in my almost 9 years of marriage and I had never heard of her. I know of her product, which is a bed, but I've never tried that brand before.

So, you might be wondering why I'm even bringing all of this up. Well, what struck me was the fact that Kirsten added a very interesting article and youtube video to look at and research. The article is about a study done on sleep and how doing something as simple as changing your mattress could make you sleep a whole lot better. The video also talks about this same study and shows you how pressure points in your body could make sleeping difficult and have you wake up with back pain.

Now, what Kirsten doesn't know, and what all of you all are about to, is that one of the many things that I used to sell was mattresses when I worked in retail management. They can be the hardest thing to sell to someone because you want to make sure that the customer doesn't feel foolish when lying on one in the showroom.

That may sound funny to any of you who have never worked retail, but it's really very true. Just go back to the last time you were shopping for a mattress and think back to how long you did the *Charmin* test when you felt the thickness of each mattress. If you actually laid on it, how long did you do that before you said, "I'll take it." Chances are, you didn't spend that long. You may have even purchased the same brand that you've had for years because it seemed like a good one.

Mattresses are a long time investment-- that is a very true statement. And you do spend about a third of your life on one. Having said that, you may be wondering which mattress I think is the best, or you may even wonder what I sleep on. And the answer to that is simple, I don't have a preference. I have what is comfortable for me. I don't suggest anything in particular to anyone because everyone is different.

I've owned only two beds in my almost 36 years of life. The first was a very flat and very firm twin mattress that I had during my childhood and early adult years. The second is the one I sleep on now which is a full size pillow top from one of those discount mattress places.

I didn't pick out either of these because they were gifts to me. The first was from my mother who purchased the best one she could find so I could start out my big girl life with a good bed. The second was from my mother in-law who purchased the best she could find so Scott and I could start out our married life with a good bed. I liked each of these beds because of their comfort level-- at least the full was comfortable before kids and cats. Now, it's a bit crowded lol!

I really can't tell you if a *Sleep Number* is the way to

go. I've never had one, I don't work for that company, and as I stated before, everyone is different.

But what I can give you is some good information on how to shop for a mattress the next time you need one. Picking the wrong mattress can spell trouble for anyone with fibro and that is certainly not how one can feel fabulous, so let's get to the tips, shall we?

Tip number one: If a fire hazard is of any concern to you because of children or smokers, the best mattress to purchase is a pillow top. You'd think that it wouldn't be, but the thickness actually helps in this case because it takes much longer to burn one. A flat firm is the absolute worst in this case and a plush didn't fair much better. The actual test was done on a television show several years back. It was a show dedicated to testing out products to see which ones really held up.

Tip number two: When shopping for a mattress, lie on each type, a flat firm, a plush, and a pillow top, for at least 10 minutes at a time BEFORE you decide which one to get. And if you sleep with a partner, make sure they do the same so you can better decide. Mattresses today are much more sophisticated and they have actually split the comfort levels for each sleeper. You can purchase a mattress that has firm on one side and plush on the other if that's to your liking.

Tip number three: Make sure you lie on the mattress the same way you do when you sleep so you can get the best idea for your comfort.

If you follow these tips, you should be able to find the best mattress for yourself. These tips won't do you much good, however, if you don't know when you should start to shop for a new mattress.

The answer is that you should start shopping for one if yours is around 10 years old or if yours is starting to show significant wear. Most mattresses will start to get big dips in the middle when they wear out. So if your cat, dog, or small child tends to disappear in the middle of your mattress, it might be time for a new one.

Small impressions are body impressions and those are a normal occurrence on a mattress. These may make the mattress look "lumpy" when you put a flat fitted sheet on the bed, but they are fine and are not signs that it's time for a new one.

Another big reason to start looking when your mattress hits its 10th birthday, is dust mites. Dust mites are inevitable, hard to get rid of, but not impossible. You can kill some of them off by deodorizing your mattress from time to time with a bit of baking soda or Borax. Just follow the labeling directions. Once they die, they can, however, stay trapped inside a mattress and cause it to become very heavy throughout the years. This is why it is suggested to shop every 10 years for a new one.

For any further information, you can check out the youtube video that Kirsten from Select Comfort passed along to me. It will give you a few other ideas about shopping for a mattress.

You might also want to take a look at the contest Select Comfort is doing between now and April 2. You can register to win a mattress from them which is pretty cool. I'm not sure if you have to become one of their mailing list members, but, to enter for a possible chance to win, that might not be so bad. I'll leave that up to you all.

Also, don't forget about the contest I'm running for a chance to win an autographed copy of *Fibromyalgia and Sex Can Be a Pain In the Neck...and back and shoulders or The Fibro Hand.* The 25th commenter (which is coming up very soon) will be the first lucky winner!

Stay Fabulous!
Love and friendship,

Kimberley

Tuesday, March 31, 2009

There's a Frenzy in April...

There is a *Frenzy* that starts tomorrow and it lasts through the entire month of April. The play writing community just loves it, but Mathew Broderick-- uh, not so much. April is the time to dust of your pencils, pens, paper, or that lap top you use as an expensive paper weight, and write to your heart's content... Or at least 100 pages of a screen play.

You might be wondering why I'm even talking about this today because it has nothing to do with fibro. And you'd be right, writing has little to do with fibro, but it has everything to do with feeling fabulous. I know that not everyone out there in the reader world is a writer, but we all have things we like to do.

Some of us like to garden, read, practice yoga, or go bike riding. Whatever you enjoy doing in your spare time is the topic for today. Now, some of you are probably saying to yourself right now as you read this, *yeah, you're crazy Kim if you think I have any spare time*. I know you are thinking that so don't try and think any different.

We all have very little time that we dedicate to ourselves because so many people depend on us. We make breakfast, lunch, and dinner every day. We feed the pets, walk the dog (or in my case, the cats--

no seriously, don't laugh-- I have to give mine exercise because he's on the pudgy side), we take care of the kids, drive the kids to soccer practice, go to the PTA meetings, make the coffee, wash the dishes, do the laundry, and whatever else that may be needed on any given day. We have a tough list to finish all day, every day, and I sometimes wonder how I've made time to brush my teeth. My days can last anywhere from 12 hours to 18, so there is really very little time for me to be me. I'm sure it's the same for all of you too.

But we shouldn't be doing this to ourselves. We matter because if we don't take some time out for ourselves every day, we can't do what we need to for others. If you have fibro, that's all the more reason to take some time. You don't need a flare to stop you in your tracks.

Carving time out in your day should be one of your priorities to keep yourself feeling fabulous. This can be a tough task when other family members are involved because sometimes they don't understand why you need time. I know it's happened to me because *I'm Mom, I don't need anything...* That card sound familiar? When my hubby tries to sneak in more free time than he should by pulling that card, I kindly remind him that I'd be more than happy to do what he wants me to do, but he needs to prepare himself for the day when I have a flare and he'll have to do **everything** on his own.

Fibro and Fabulous

He might not like the gentle reminder that he's just as capable to do chores, but I'm sure he'd rather hear that then do **all** the chores on his own-- I know I would. I do the same with my oldest too and I try hard not to feel guilty about it because, after all, they make time for themselves, so why shouldn't I?

Script Frenzy is my way of giving myself permission to take some time for myself. It's a way where I can carve out an hour a day, or a few hours in the week, just for me. It will be a tough challenge to carve out enough time to complete a 100 page script, but I think I can do it. But even if I don't, I am still a winner because I'm taking time out of my day to feel fabulous.

So, why don't we all try a challenge to give ourselves some time to relax. You do whatever tickles your fancy, it doesn't have to be about a 100 page script. It can be anything you want, just try and track it for yourself in a journal or on the calendar so you can look back on April as a fabulous month.

Contest Update: We are just 6 comments away from a winner so keep the comments coming!

Stay Fabulous!
Love and friendship,

Kimberley

Tuesday, May 12, 2009

Irritation On Awareness Day

Wow it's been some time since my last post! I'm truly sorry about that. I try to post for all of you at least once a week no matter how I feel because I think it's important to help people as much as I can with this debilitating disease. I know that I may not know as much as some people, but I try to help with what I can.

April was a tough month for me because of a flare. My fibro can be a bit wacky when it comes to flares because sometimes I will only get pain and other times I will have a ton of other problems all at once. This flare has a huge amount of problems with it from insomnia, fibro fog, pain, fatigue, anxiety, depression, and eczema and seborrheic dermatitis skin irritations. I'm still having problems, but I am feeling a little better with the fatigue-- hence the post.

This post is going to be about skin irritations because they are really bugging me today so I thought it'd be a good one to discuss. About half of fibro patients suffer from some kind of skin irritation, disorder, or disease. There are many different kinds and one in particular is called eczema.

Eczema has many different severities to it. They

range from topical dermatitis, something generally diagnosed with people who show reactions to some type of soap or detergents, to seborrheic dermatitis which is an oil gland disorder. It is typically diagnosed in people that have eczema around the eye(s). I was born with this type and it is never fun when you have this kind of skin flare.

Way back when, some now 36 years ago, there was nothing that could be put on the eye for relief because topical medications were not meant for the eyes. Over the counter anti-itch treatments like cortisone are usually not recommended either because they can cause blindness if they get into the eyes.

When I was little, my eyes didn't bother me so much, but once I got into my twenties, this seborrheic dermatitis would surround my eyes. I tried some eye creams out on the market and got a little bit of relief. I would have to switch brands every once in a while if one in particular stopped working, but all-in-all, they generally worked for several years. Eventually though, I would find that the annoyance would come back harder and stronger. By my late twenties I stopped using makeup to elevate irritation.

The elimination of makeup helped greatly, until now. So far I have eliminated every cleaning product, detergent, and soap that had any type of scent to it from my daily routines. I started to wear gloves when cleaning or doing the dishes and I dust and run the vacuum two to three times a week to relieve any other irritants that may be causing this flare.

I don't wear makeup anymore, and as of late, I have limited my wheat and cheese intake from my diet just to see if I'm all of the sudden allergic to that. So far nothing right now seems to be working.

Showering has become very painful and I often wish I didn't have to bathe at all, but that of course, isn't really an option when you live with others. It probably isn't a good idea period since every one of us has to be in contact with another human being every once in a while. And somehow, being a recluse doesn't sound appealing either.

So what does one do at this point? Well, I guess I'll be taking yet another trip to the doctor, but at least this time I'll be seeing a dermatologist instead of a rheumotolgist. I hope that we can get to the bottom of this and find out exactly what is bothering me instead of just treating the problem. I of course will keep you updated on the progress, but until then, I'd like to give you all some info I've come across while trying to help myself, hopefully, it can help some of you.

Milk and wheat can be triggers for eczema, as well as, perfumed soaps, detergents, and shampoos and conditioners. Other allergen triggers that may cause problems are cigarette smoke, makeup products, cleaning products, mold, mildew, and pet dander.

Some things that may help elevate your skin symptoms are stress relief techniques, like deep breathing or even yoga, moisturizers that are perfume and dye free, herbal supplements like evening primrose oil, st john's wart, and vitamin b-12, drinking plenty of water, ultra violet light from either the sun or tanning beds, and bathing in baking soda may also help too.

A couple of sites to look at for further information are the National Eczema Association and Skin Deep: Cosmetic Safety Reviews. Both will give you helpful information. The National Eczema Association offers a free news letter that is sent to your email on useful info for eczema sufferers.

Skin Deep will tell you the severity of chemicals and irritants a product has. It is a pretty extensive site and some of the products that are severely irritating to the skin may surprise you because there are supposed "all-natural" products with a questionable label. Some of them have a high rating of chemicals and skin irritants in them. The ratings go from 1 to 10, 10 being the most severe.

The FDA does not regulate makeup and other health and beauty aid products and this makes it hard for a consumer to know what they are really buying. Skin Deep is a non-profit organization that tests a good majority of the popular products out there and will let you know what's in it. They don't have every product that's out there on the market today, but they have a lot.

I hope some of this helps you all out there on this wonderful Fibro Awareness Day. Take care of yourselves, be fabulous, and don't scratch lol!

Stay Fabulous!
Love and friendship,

Kimberley

Thursday, May 14, 2009

My Frustrations Runath Over

I finally found a doctor that was excepting new patients for my eczema swelling. He was a general practitioner and I had doubts about seeing a GP because they really don't have a specific field of expertise-- especially when it comes to fibro patients. But I went anyway because I needed some relief from my swollen eyes.

The nurse came in first and asked a lot of questions about my skin condition and I gave her my entire medical history in about 5 minutes of conversation. Being a fibro patient has some perks and having a knack to spew out 36 years of medical history in 5 minutes is one of them.

The doctor came in after a few minutes and then asked to see my hands and face. I showed him and then he asked if I was using new moisturizer. I told him that I have been changing my moisturizer constantly because nothing is giving me relief. The last "new" moisturizer was something that I've been using for about a month.

He told me to stop using it and go with baby oil and said I'm having an allergic reaction. He gave me a script for steroids and some kind of soap and then sent me on my way. It took him longer to write out the script then it did to talk to me and I REALLY hate doctors like that. Now granted, it was almost 5 PM and he wanted to go home-- in fact he left the same time we did, but I really don't think that is an excuse for sweeping my health conditions under the rug.

Doctors are like the rest of us--they are human and have families they want to go home to, but they also have an oath. My advice to people is to only go to a GP if you have the sniffles. I know that may sound harsh, but I've seen enough of them in my past to know that they don't have a clue about people and what they go through with serious health conditions. The only thing I've seen with GP's is that they are good with colds and the flu.

I'm also finding as of late that I need to argue with doctors a lot more just to get the medical attention I need and that's really not fair considering they make more in an hour than I did all day at my job as a retail manager. In fact, I had to work all week just to get what they make in an hour.

I don't mean to make this into a rant that is bashing doctors in general-- that's not the point-- please don't misunderstand. What I'm saying is that if you have a problem with your skin, find a dermatologist. If you have an autoimmune problem, see a rheumatologist.

Specialists seem to be the way to go and that's sad really because specialists can get really expensive. I know I was paying a lot out of pocket when I first started seeing them-- and I had insurance. It didn't cover anything, but I had insurance. Alternative care is usually out of pocket too. Right now, out of pocket is really out of reach for most of us because we live in *the land of free* to pay what others deem as a fair price.

I hope that somebody out there someday changes the health industry and makes it better for the patients instead of it being better for the insurance and drug companies. These pill pushers need to be pushed out of the office and make room for the ones who are willing to treat the whole person.

As for me, I'll be making an appointment with a dermatologist tomorrow and probably start my research into finding a specialist for allergies. Hope you are all Fabulous and don't forget about the contest.

Stay Fabulous!
Love and friendship,

Kimberley

Tuesday, May 26, 2009

Summertime Recipes

Chicken Salad

Summertime can bring a lot of fun for a family, but it can also bring flares because of the hot days and cool nights. Cooking is hard to do in the summer because temperatures rise and having flares can make things worse.

But we all have to eat! And when you have Fibro, you have to eat well in order to *stay fabulous*. I'm going to share some new recipes that are not in the book *The Fibro Hand* recipe section. These two recipes are quick and easy and you won't have turn on your stove-- unless you want to of course!

The first recipe is a new spin on an old summer favorite, Chicken Salad. I often make it with left over pieces of the prior night's roaster chicken, but you can very easily use readymade chicken breast strips from the meat section of your local market, or you can also brown a couple of breasts for this easy recipe too.

What you will need:

4 cups of shredded chicken breast (about a breast and half cooked)

4 tablespoons of mayonnaise

3 tablespoons of fresh chopped basil

2 teaspoons of paprika

1-2 teaspoons (to taste) of sea salt

15 pitted kalamata olives in olive oil

2 Roma tomatoes

3 small cloves of garlic (chopped)

Mix all the ingredients together and serve cold and with your favorite crackers or bread. This amount of salad will easily make about 8 sandwiches.

Spinach Dip

Spinach Dip is one of my favorite snacks. This recipe is really easy and really good with wheat crackers or chips.

What you will need:

3 tablespoons of softened cream cheese

12 ounces of sour cream

4 small cloves of chopped garlic

1 slice of a purple onion chopped

1 chopped Roma tomato

8 ounces of chopped frozen spinach

1 medium green pepper (diced)

1/2 cup of grated Romano and Parmesan cheese

1 teaspoon of sea salt

Directions:

1.) Sauté spinach, tomatoes, garlic, onion, and pepper with one tablespoon of Canola oil until softened (about 5 minutes).

2.) Blend sour cream, cream cheese, grated cheese, sea salt, and sauté mixture together.

3.) Chill for one hour and serve with wheat crackers, chips, or tortilla chips.

Hope you enjoy these summer favorites of mine!

Stay Fabulous!
Love and friendship,

Kimberley

P.S. Fibro and Fabulous is now boasting its own domain thanks to all of you readers! Yeah!

P.S.S. We are only 5 comments away from a winner... will that winner be you? Post a comment to make sure you are in the running!

I've decided to add this entry more so because of the comment that was made from a cherished reader. Trisha is a lot like all of us, she feels bad that her partner is taking on the brunt of the financial burdens of life. She can't work more than 4 hours a couple of days a week at a conventional job.

I truly feel her pain because I know EXACTLY what she is going through. It's not fun, and at times, it can feel down, right ugly. You feel like a bum, a worthless individual, and that's the farthest thing from fabulous that you can feel. It's also the farthest from the truth.

None of us should feel this way. We are all capable of making some beautiful contributions to society, our family, our friends, and to the bills, if we so choose. We fibromites may not be able to do EVERYTHING that healthy people can do in a day, but we CAN do it. We just may need more time to do it in, and if we are provided that extra time, we usually can outperform our healthy counterparts because we do it better!

I hope that you find a way to feel fabulous at work sometime soon, Trisha. It's hard, I know, it took me a long time to find a way to feel fabulous too. A non-conventional job did the trick for me and I'm very happy writing and doing sales in legal insurance. It might be different for you. I will continue to think good thoughts for you and your partner and hope that you both make it through this difficult time.

Sales are not for everyone, I know. I do sales because I can help people that need me. You may find that something else works better for you. The only bit of advice I can offer is to try and find something that you can be passionate about.

I used to sell paint for a living. Yeah, it didn't pay all of the bills, but it paid for some. It was fun for me because I knew I wasn't pressuring anyone into buying something they didn't need-- why? Statistically, they never entered my department unless they planned on buying paint in the first place.

Selling is not easy, you have to believe in a product and then believe that you can sell it. It's not for everyone. I will keep you and your darling fiancé in my thoughts and I hope you find what makes you feel fabulous very soon.

Fibro and Fabulous

Thursday, August 20, 2009

Pam Gaulin in emFirst for Women/em magazine

When you have fibro, you sometimes have to get creative when it comes to paying your bills...

Don't get me wrong-- some people can have a job before diagnoses and manage to keep it. But most of us need to find ways to maintain our health and wallet by looking for ways to work from home.

This article is about three work from home options--- AND YES, they are definitely legit. I have done 2 out of the 3 listed for quite a few years now, and I agree with the magazine's take on the pros and cons.

My father always used to say, "Do what you love, the money will come." and he's right. Of course he also used to say, "You won't get rich working retail, but it pays the bills." I can't agree with him on the later-- retail only pays some of the bills, but it was a job for me BF (Before Fibro).

Sometimes we fibromites can feel useless because we have no energy to perform at a job, but we shouldn't! Especially when there are places out there where you can make some money and feel accomplished.

Stay fabulous!

Love and friendship,

Kimberley

Pam Gaulin in *First for Women* magazine

A Girl's Best Friend

Diamonds have always been known as a girl's best friend. The coin phrase was first performed by Carol Channing in the 1949 broadway production Gentlemen Prefer Blonds. However, it was made famous when actress Maryilyn Monroe sang it for the 1953 film version of the broadway play.

The diamond is known as the king of the crystals because it was believed to instill trust, love, and harmony in relationships if given out freely. It's no wonder that they are a popular favorite for engagement rings.

The history of the diamond makes it understandable that it could be a girl's best friend, but did you ever think it could aid you in clearing out the fog from your mind? Could this king of the crystals also be a fibromite's best friend? Research taken from the book Love Is In The Earth: A Kaleidoscope Of Crystals indicates that our ancestors used this stone to help them maintain a clear head towards the path of enlightenment. If this is the case, the diamond can be looked at in a whole new way.

I've discussed meditation in a previous blog where I've given you some tips on how to clear your mind out of some of the stress and clutter that builds up from the day by giving you some examples of how I cheat in my meditations. I sometimes need something to look at, like the light of a candle, or a tropical fish because my fog-filled mind can race with thoughts.

This blog entry will discuss meditation, but it's a meditation of a different kind. This is called Crystal Meditation and it can lessen the severity of your pain from Fibromyalgia. Now before you start thinking that I'm going off the new age deep end, let me explain a little about crystals and how we use them almost every day without thinking about it.

Crystals, rocks, and minerals are a part of our life. They are as common as the trees, grass, and plants. We use them to run our compact disc players, we accessorize our outfits with them, we nourish our bodies with them, and we use them in medications to help us feel better. Crystals are very common in everyday use.

Crystals used to be made into elixirs many years ago for countless numbers of aliments. Some herbalists and witches still use this practice today, however, modern medicine usually breaks the crystal down for its properties and puts them into pill form. For instance, the crystal known as sodalite has been used in some medications for depression. Sodalite can also help with insomnia and some digestive disorders.

Even though some people still use the practice of making elixirs, it is not something one should do without the help of someone knowledgeable. Certain

crystals are lethal in an elixir form, malachite, is one
of them.

You should also discuss this with your doctor too,
because some crystal elixirs may interfere with the
medications or supplements you are already taking. I
strongly urge any of you to do extensive research
before partaking in this old practice.

Elixirs are not the only way to reap the benefits of a
crystal's properties. You can use them in meditation
and use them for healing. Crystal healing is the
simple practice of placing a stone on the infected
area. If you want clarity for the mind, for instance,
you can not only use a diamond, but you can use
stones like clear quartz, pearl, and opal.

Other crystals can be used to alleviate headaches,
joint pain, or digestive problems. I especially like
Blue Lace Agate for autoimmune conditions like
arthritis and Fibromyalgia.

Meditation with a crystal can be as simple as
imagining your pain in the form of a sphere,
releasing it from your body, and absorbing it into the
crystal. You can meditate as elaborate as you want,
or as simple as you want with this exercise.

The nice part about this exercise is that you can use
it with or without the crystal near you. I remember
one time I was running late for work and I had
forgotten my Blue Lace Agate. I used to use it very

often when I worked retail because the calming effects it would give me during stressful times did wonders to get me through the day. Sometimes, just rubbing the stone while it was in my pocket was all I needed to be as pain free as possible.

The day I had forgotten it was a trying one. I had to move a ton of stock to the sales floor. My back felt like someone was stabbing me with little needles all morning and all afternoon, until I remembered that I didn't have to feel that way. All I had to do was focus on the stone and some of that pain could be avoided all together. I started to focus on the stone and my pain level started to decrease.

For best results, it is suggested that you reconnect with the stone and hold it on the affected area for about 5 minutes when possible. This will absorb the pain energy into the stone and keep it from recycling through you.

Stay fabulous!

Love and friendship,

Kimberley

A different form of healing is in the form of a meditation that is most commonly referred to as chakra alignment or chakra balancing. I learned this form of therapy many years back from a friend, well before I was ever diagnosed with Fibromyalgia. At the time, I was suffering from migraines, due to my wisdom teeth, and I also suffered back pain, due to a back injury in a dance class.

I listened to her, but a lot had gotten lost in the translation. I was very naive when it came to old world belief systems in my early twenties. Catholic schooling at an early age put a huge damper on my learning of old customs and religions because most of the priests and nuns considered other religions a work of the devil. The priests and nuns were great in my middle school and high school-- don't get me wrong, they were just a little too rigid in their belief system to help me.

A book called *Chakra Clearing* by Dorren Virtue broke me of that nagging feeling of being sent to hell for my sins of looking elsewhere for relief. I liked this book for many reasons, but the few that stand out were the exercises, the ease of the read, and the book cover.

Now, some of you may wonder why I like the book cover so much. The answer to that is that I use it in my meditations. Why? Well, there are some days where I just can't seem to concentrate very well and the cover reminds me of what colors are where on the body. Put plainly, I use it as a cheat sheet.

The exercises are nice too because they allowed me to relax long enough to find out which part of my body needed attention and which parts were just along for the ride in my pain factors. Believe it or not, it can be hard to determine what really hurts.

Some people that have injured a disk will have leg pain, a common problem in back pain sufferers. At times, the leg pain can be more of a problem than the back pain. This is where quieting one's self is key, however, it can be difficult for people to distinguish the root of their pain if they find it hard to quite themselves.

I'm one of those people that can't quite themselves long enough. I need to be able to do something-- even when I'm trying to relax. It's very hard for me to be completely relaxed with anything in life and this is why I tend to need visual aide when it comes to meditation. I also retain more of the information in a book if it is presented simply. It's very hard for me to read a book that sounds too much like my high school text books. I find it very hard to keep focused, I need straight talk.

The version of the book that I have is rather old. It was printed in 1998. It is still available, however, and there are also newer versions. If you want to learn about your body's light patterns and vibrations and how to fix them so they work properly, get a copy of the book. It's a great read and may help you in alleviating some of your Fibromyalgia pain.

Stay fabulous!

Love and friendship,

Kimberley

I couldn't finish this book without talking about one last subject. It's about partners and the role they play in our feeling fabulous. There are some partners that really understand us and know what we are dealing with, there are some that are absolutely clueless, but help us cope, and there are some that can't deal with anything. The ones that can't deal are usually the ones that have too many of their own problems.

Some of you may think I'm being harsh, but I'm not. We've all come across people in our BF (before Fibro) and AD (After Diagnoses) lives that are drama queens (kings). They can't deal with you and your illness because that's *your drama,* not theirs. Drama queens (and kings) like to create drama in their life so people can feel sorry for them. It's their way of coping with the world.

There's no way to compete with someone like that and I don't even think it's worth trying to because those types of people can suck the life right out of you-- not something you need when you are already fatigued. If those types of people want out of your life, so be it. Chalk it up to them "watching too much *Dynasty"* and move onto associating yourself with people that care about how YOU feel.

Below is an article I came across in the recent news. It's a survey that was taken on Fibromyalgia patients and their marriages. The article does not paint a pretty picture to say the least, the numbers are very startling.

One would think that this kind of thing is happening more often than not, but remember, this is only one survey and there are no real numbers here. You don't know how many people participated, how many had marital problems to begin with, if the partners were in a long or short term marriage, etc., etc.

I don't like articles like this at all. This is another clear-cut case of an author writing an article to suit her opinion and that's just not fair to all of us. Articles need to be based on facts and if you are writing an article about one... BACK YOUR FACTS UP. We don't even know where the survey is coming from. We only know that his name is Ray.

I will add the article at the bottom of this blog here so you can all come to your own conclusions. You now know how I feel, I think partners, friends, relatives, and co-workers that get it are fabulous and more writing should be done on them. They are brave souls and unsung heroes that need to be recognized for their greatness. Here's to hoping that you all find the unsung heroes in your lives!

http://chronicfatigue.about.com/b/2009/11/07/has-your-marriage-been-damaged-by-fibromyalgia-or-chronic-fatigue-syndrome.htm

Stay Fabulous!

Love and friendship,

Kimberley

Fibro and Fabulous

Afterword...

This concludes the first print edition of *Fibro and Fabulous*. I truly hope that you enjoyed it as much as I had putting it together. This book was truly a labor of love and I could not have written it without all of you, my cherished readers.

You are the back bone of this blog and book. You keep me going when I feel I have nothing left to give. You are my reasons for getting up in the morning and writing and I can't thank you enough for that!

Love,

Kimberley

About the Author...

Kimberley has lived in Connecticut almost all of her life. She lives with her husband, two daughters, two cats, two frogs, and several tropical fish and plants. She loves a good book, cooking, practicing yoga, gardening, crocheting, baking, and the video games *Fable* and *Castlevania*. In her spare time, Kimberley likes to watch wrestling and has been known to do a little karaoke every now and again. She is the author of three books on the disease known as Fibromyalgia. Kimberley has also author many articles on the subject in addition to her popular blog. She is also an active member of many different forums dedicated to Fibromyalgia and Chronic Fatigue.

Kimberley has over 27 years of experience in writing and has published in several other different genres. She has received many rewards for her writing achievements. Some of her achievements include a nomination for *Best Poets of the 90's,* as well as, *One of the Best Poets* of the year in 2007. She is also one of *Cambridge Who's Who among Executive and Professional Women.* Go to www.kimberleylinstruth-beckom.com and www.fibroandfabulous.com for more information about the author. See www.lulu.com/isis1lotus for information on purchasing any of Kimberley's other books.

Other books by the author
The Fibro Hand
Fibromyalgia and Sex Can Be a Pain in the
Neck...and back and shoulders
The Puzzle Called Life
Blue Water Baptism
The Mommy Times

Fibro and Fabulous

Fibro and Fabulous

Fibro and Fabulous

www.ingramcontent.com/pod-product-compliance
Lightning Source LLC
Chambersburg PA
CBHW022129080426
42734CB00006B/282